PIZZAS

Indo-Pak Kebabs

PIZZA - PASTA - KEBAB

LOUNGE

COFFEE SHOP

PIZZAS
KEBABS
CURRIES

HIPS

MADE
S
VAY

CHINESE
TAKE-AWAY

FREE HOUSE

AN'S

856

BREWERS

FISH & CHIPS

SNOOKER CLUB

AP
CING

HOWS

ONE

TAKEAWAY
DELIVERY
SITTING IN

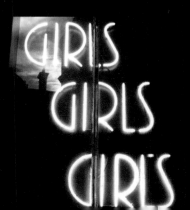

GIRLS

GIRLS

GIRLS

Rebus's **Scotland**

'He's out there driving through the

night, an exile on Princes Street,

stopping off at pubs across Edinburgh.

He always ends up at the Oxford Bar

on Young Street, waiting for me

to walk through the door with another

episode for him.'

Rebus's Scotland

Ian Rankin

A Personal Journey

photographed by Tricia Malley
and Ross Gillespie

ORION

To Giles Gordon
to whom all things seemed possible

First published in hardback in Great Britain in 2005 by
Orion Books
an imprint of the Orion Publishing Group Ltd
Orion House, 5 Upper St Martin's Lane,
London WC2H 9EA

10 9 8 7 6 5 4 3 2 1

A CIP catalogue record for this book is available
from the British Library.

ISBN: 0 75285 245 0

Designed by Harry Green

Printed in Great Britain by Butler & Tanner, Frome and London

www.orionbooks.co.uk

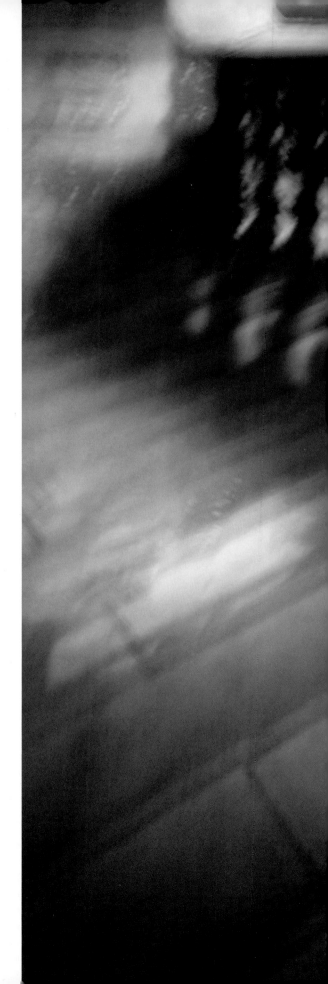

PAGE 1 View from a holding-cell, St Leonard's.

Contents

It requires great love of it deeply to read

The configuration of a land,

Gradually grow conscious of fine shadings,

Of great meanings in slight symbols

HUGH MACDIARMID, 'SCOTLAND'

In the first room there is a birth,

in another a death, in a third a sordid

drinking-bout, and the detective

and the Bible-reader cross upon the stairs

ROBERT LOUIS STEVENSON, *PICTURESQUE NOTES*

1

Court and Spark

ONCE I HAD CUT THE RIBBON, it was official: Ian Rankin Court existed.

This was the August of 2004. I'd been contacted earlier in the year by the housebuilder, asking my agreement in the naming of the street. I'd argued that Rankin Court or maybe even Rebus Court would be more seemly, but he'd managed to persuade me otherwise.

Friends who knew I was coming back to Cardenden for the ceremony had already alerted me to the six-figure prices attached to this new housing development, sited where a builder's yard had once stood. Six figures: and none of our parents had even owned their own homes. I was shown around the development. Some of the gardens backed on to a trickling stream. It ran through the Den, an area of overgrown wilderness we had all been taken to on primary school outings. Denend Primary sat just the other side of the railway bridge. I'd won my first literary prize of any kind thanks to my primary school. In my final year at High School, I'd been sent back to Denend to 'shadow' one of the teachers – just in case it gave me a taste for the profession. (It didn't.) One day, however, among the morning announcements I saw mention of a nationwide poetry contest. I decided to enter, wrote a poem called 'Euthanasia' for the occasion . . . and won second prize.

Plenty of water had trickled through the Den since then, and a lot had changed in the town of my youth. I'd arrived ahead of schedule, driving from Edinburgh. With over half an hour to spare, I'd decided to revisit the cul-de-sac where I'd grown up. It's called Craigmead Terrace, and the Rankins had lived at number 17 from the year it was built (1960; also the year I was born) until my father's death in 1990. The front garden of our old home had become a parking space, but other-wise the street seemed little different. The same could not be said of the damp and unlovely flats in the streets behind, which had disappeared,

Cardenden: smoke still rises
from one chimney, but the winding-wheel
is all that's left of the colliery.

replaced by terraced housing. Auchterderran Junior High, which I'd attended for a couple of my teenage years, was no longer a school. And my village had ceased to have its own postal identity many years before. As a kid, I'd known the place as Bowhill. It formed part of what old-timers called the ABCD – Auchterderran, Bowhill, Cardenden and Dundonald. The four distinct parishes had become one – Cardenden – in the early 1970s, as far as the authorities were concerned. This had been at a time, I seem to remember, when there had been further plans to split the Kingdom of Fife in half, with the northern section coming under Dundee's remit, and the southern part owing allegiance to Edinburgh. A fierce local campaign was launched, with the blessing of famously anti-royalist MP Willie Hamilton, and Fife – 'the Kingdom of Fife' – was eventually saved.

You'll find Fife, one-time seat of the King of Scotland, on any map of the British Isles. Sandwiched between Dundee and Edinburgh, it is shaped like a terrier's head, an accident of topography which thrilled me as a child. That aspect alone gave Fife an individual identity: our county at least *looked* like something. Later on, I learned that Fifers were seen as being different from other Scots. One saying from folklore had it that 'ye need a lang spune to sup wi' a Fifer'. I think this means we are close-knit . . . or maybe just keen to hold on to what we've got. (The same thing is said, incidentally, and again in Scots folklore, of the Devil.) The region of Scotland of which Fife is part was in ancient times known as Fib, which can, of course, also mean a lie, and Fifers have always been great storytellers, relishing the opportunity to make their tales fantastical or supernatural. At High School, I'd undertaken a geography project on the history of coal-mining in Fife, and had speculated that the word 'Carden' (from which Cardenden takes its name) might have related to a den of witches, since the Scots word for a witch is 'car'. Wishful thinking on my teenage part, I'm bound to say, but something I would come back to in my use of superstition and folk tales in my first published novel, *The Flood*.

That morning in Cardenden, still with time to spare before the ribbon-cutting, I'd stopped the car by the roadside, unable for a moment to believe that the church where I'd been christened – St Fothad's – had vanished, a new house appearing in its place. St Fothad's had played a vital role in my early life. I'd gone to Sunday School there, leaving my mother and sister in the pew as I was taken downstairs with the other bairns to sing songs about building houses on sand and rowing boats ashore. Later, I'd won a prize by having a perfect attendance in one kirk year. Indeed, the stamps in my attendance-card had been wrongly assigned, giving me fifty-three attendances out of a possible fifty-two.

And now St Fothad's was gone. St Fothad's where, it was said, centuries back one visitor had marvelled at how the poor of the parish were offered not food but pieces of black rock to provide them with warmth . . . It seemed to me telling: if churches (and with them a large portion of their meaning and history) could disappear, then so could – and probably would – everything else. After all, there were no more coal-mines, and the 'bings' (our term for slag-heaps) had been flattened and landscaped. Heading towards Denend, however, I was astonished to find that one seemingly flimsy artefact from my childhood did remain. Near the primary school sat a narrow shack, constructed, so far as I could tell, from sheets of corrugated iron. This had been where, fully forty years before, June Jarvis, a close friend to my eldest sister, would cut my hair. Back then, it had seemed a building not meant to last, yet here it was. Practically every other shop and building in the town had changed ownership, or been replaced with something more modern, but this hairdresser's remained. On arriving at Ian Rankin Court, I felt compelled to mention this to someone.

'Aye,' they said, 'and it's still June Jarvis that runs it.'

June Jarvis in her hairdresser's shop.

John Rebus grew up in Cardenden. In fact, he grew up in Bowhill, in the same cul-de-sac as me, if the books are to be believed:

> Rebus had been born in a pre-fab but brought up
> in a terrace much like this one   (*Dead Souls,* p 36).

In *The Black Book* we learn that Rebus's father was born in a miners' row. My own father's family had lived in just such a house, built quickly and in long rows to identical designs. These were thrown up in

order to get as many men into the area as possible early in the twenti-eth century, when the demand for coal seemed insatiable:

> Cardenden had grown up around coal, hurried streets constructed in the twenties and thirties to house the incoming miners. These streets hadn't even been given names, just numbers. Rebus's family had moved into 13th Street. Relocation had taken the family to a pre-fab in Cardenden, and from there to a terraced house in a cul-de-sac in Bowhill   (*Dead Souls*, p 306).

This was my family's own trajectory, though I think my father had actually lived on 17th Street rather than 13th. I was born in a pre-fab in Cardenden, my parents moving us to Craigmead Terrace immedi-ately after it was built. All the same, Rebus's past is inextricably linked to my own, and this can sometimes cause problems. For example, in *The Black Book* I say that Rebus went to school in Cowdenbeath. By the time we reach *Dead Souls*, some six years later, we find that he actually attended Auchterderran Secondary School, and left at fifteen to enlist in the Army. Both cannot be true, and comprise a conflation of my own education. I spent the first two years of my high school education at Auchterderran, then was offered a place at Beath Senior High in Cow-denbeath. (The brightest few kids were decanted from all the Junior Highs in the area: one friend, cleverer than me in most subjects, chose not to switch, a decision which surely coloured his whole life there-after.) In using my own life as a template for some of Rebus's back-ground, errors sometimes do creep in. I even had to be careful over the naming of Auchterderran: in Rebus's time, it was a Secondary School; by the time I arrived there, its status had been altered to Junior High – a blessing, in that the badge on the breast-pocket of the school blazer no longer bore the letters ASS.

Here is Rebus on the west-central Fife of the early 1990s:

> Like the towns and villages around it, Cowdenbeath looked and felt depressed: closed down shops and drab chainstore clothes. But he knew that the people were stronger than their situation might suggest. Hardship bred a bitter, quickfire humour and a resilience to

all but the most terminal of life's tragedies. He didn't like to think about it too deeply, but inside he felt like he really was 'coming home'. Edinburgh might have been his base for twenty years, but he was a Fifer. 'Fly Fifers', some people called them. Rebus was ready to do battle with some very fly people indeed (*Dead Souls*, p 127).

I've said in the past that I started writing the Rebus books in order to make sense of Edinburgh, my adopted home. But Fife plays a major role in several of Rebus's adventures, and comprises the majority of his memories. I wonder now if all this time, I've really been trying to make sense of my own upbringing, in order better to understand myself.

Not that Rebus is me, of course, and the title of this book – *Rebus's Scotland* – is a trick typical of a novelist. Since Rebus is not real, how can the country where he lives be real? The only way to make sense of my fictional universe is to say something of myself, showing how my autobiography merges with his, and how my sense of Scotland and Scottishness becomes his. This then is a story of the relationship between Rebus, his creator, and the country called Scotland. It can't be a guide-book (I lack the skills), nor can it be a history book. There are plenty of excellent examples of both on the shelves of many book-shops, and I may quote from a few along the way.

I've already played another trick, of course, in that Rebus was born not in Cardenden but in a bed-sit at 24 Arden Street, in the Marchmont district of Edinburgh, in the March of 1985. I was a postgraduate student at the University of Edinburgh. As well as doing research towards my thesis (on the works of novelist Muriel Spark) I was also kept busy teaching some undergraduate classes and reviewing books for a local radio station.

And trying to be a writer.

I'd had some success with my short stories, coming runner-up to the famed Iain Crichton Smith in a competition organised by *The Scotsman* newspaper. (The prize, a Sinclair Spectrum computer, had led to sleep-less nights in Arden Street as I tried to complete the game 'Hungry Horace'.) I'd also won a contest run by Radio Forth, for a story based on a true incident from my family's history (concerning a hard-drinking

LEFT: Arden Street.   ABOVE: Marchmont tenements.

uncle who had stripped off one day and wandered the Sunday after-noon streets of Lochgelly). A further anecdote, concerning an aunt who had fallen into a stream as a young girl, provided me with the opening chapter for what became a novel entitled *The Flood*. In March, just as I was finding out that *The Flood* had been accepted for publication, I got the idea for a story called *Knots and Crosses*, which would feature a detective called John Rebus.

The idea came to me as I sat by the fire in my student digs. My bed-sit would have been the original living-room of the ground-floor flat. It was spacious and high-ceilinged and freezing. There was a single bed, and a desk and chair by the large bay window. As I sat staring into the fire's gas-flames, the pun 'knots and crosses' came to me, and with it the notion that someone might be sending someone else little teasing puzzles in the shapes of knotted pieces of string and matchstick crosses.

Old College, Edinburgh.

It didn't take me long to decide that the recipient would be a cop, the sender someone from his past, some nemesis bent on his destruction. I was no great reader of detective fiction, though as a teenager I'd gone through most of the *Shaft* books (being not old enough to see their cinema versions – I was eleven when the first film was released), and been hooked on the usual slew of TV cop shows such as *Kojak, Softly Softly* and *The Sweeney*. I was, however, interested in Scots Gothic and ballads, having been sidetracked slightly in my research by Muriel Spark's use of the supernatural and her borrowings from Scotland's dark history. I'd devoured *Dr Jekyll and Mr Hyde* and James Hogg's *Confessions of a Justified Sinner*. My novel *The Flood* had attempted to use some of these devices to make something mythic of my hometown of Cardenden (renamed Carsden to reinforce the link with witchcraft). Now, I would be able to write about the darker side of Edinburgh, past and present, by using a detective as my hero.

The way I tell it in my diary of the time, Rebus appeared almost fully formed from the outset. I gave him a self-consciously playful name (a rebus is a picture-puzzle) because I was reading a lot of semiotic and deconstructionist nonsense at the time as part of my studies. The plot demanded that his brother be a stage hypnotist, so I made his father a hypnotist, too. My own father, on the other hand, had worked in a

Salisbury Crags.

grocer's shop most of his life, switching to an office job at Rosyth Dockyard in later years. Tellingly, Rebus's mother died when he was young. I'd lost my own mother when I was eighteen, and channelled my loss to him. From the start, it was clear to me that Rebus would share much of my background, growing up in the same place. In this way, we were both outsiders in Edinburgh – though at least no one muttered 'bloody student' in his direction when he entered and left a bar.

Knots and Crosses opens with Rebus standing by his father's grave in the cemetery at Cardenden. The date is 28 April, which just happens to be my birthday. Rebus isn't exactly thrilled to be back in Fife, 'where the old days had never been "the good old days" . . . how Rebus hated it all, this singular lack of an environment'. I wish I could have told the twenty-four-year old me to lighten up. Cardenden might have been rough, as were most the surrounding towns, but my own childhood was settled and safe. I would visit a friend's farm till dusk, returning home with the knees of my trousers stained green from playing foot-ball. There would be long walks into the wasteland around the coal-mine, to smoke furtive cigarettes in the long grass, and Saturday trips to Kirkcaldy to bluff our way into X-certificate films. Bowhill had its own cinema; in fact, it had two, sitting side by side, but only one ever seemed to be open. The Rex in particular was like something from the Bauhaus movement, and these days would doubtless boast a preserva-tion order. (It's long since demolished.) By the age of fourteen I was tall enough to pass for an adult, and for a time could be found there every week, glued to dodgy double bills of kung fu, horror, or English sauce. (It proved to be no hindrance that the woman who took the ticket money was a pal's mum, and hence fully cognisant of my real age.)

Betting shops, bars and barbers: this was the town of my youth. It was a scarred but rural setting. I don't recall ever seeing any bird-life more exotic than a sparrow or thrush; maybe a robin in winter. No chaffinches or magpies or blue tits, despite the long country walks we would take. Either they were steering clear of the pollution, or else I just didn't have the eyes to see. The total population of the ABCD was only around 7,000, and everyone really did seem to know everybody else. Doors would be left unlocked so visitors could walk straight in,

this practice extending to complete strangers at New Year. Two doors away from me, at number 21, lived my Uncle Math and Aunt Lizzie. Across the back fence lived one of my father's brothers, while another lived elsewhere in the town. It felt like growing up in a tribe: comforting on the one hand, but potentially stifling on the other. At least three of my aunts were called Jen or Jenny, the pot of potential first names seemingly low, perhaps for fear that an 'odd' name would make one stand out from the extended tribe.

I gave John Rebus few such confusions. Their mother having died when they were not yet in their teens, Rebus and his brother Michael were raised by their father. Rebus does not seem to have made friends easily. *Dead Souls* shows us Rebus in his final year at Secondary School. His best friend is called Mitch, and he also has a girlfriend called Janice. In returning to Cardenden in the present, to help Janice search for her missing son, Rebus is able to reflect on the town and his own past. He remembers his father drinking at the Goth (as my own father did with his circle of cronies). He also recalls a scarf with the Taj Mahal on it, which his father brought back from World War Two (as did my own father), and a scar on his father's knee which turned out not to have been a battle wound. Again, my own father sported just such a scar, and made up a story for me in which it became a memento of war.

But I had no friend called Mitch; and I didn't leave school at fifteen to join the Army. In fact, being almost a generation younger than Rebus, it would have been impossible for me to leave school at his age, the government having raised the leaving-age in the interim. I may share some of my memories with Rebus, but we are far from being the same person, and we do not inhabit the same Scotland. Doing the job he does, he tends to deal with victims and the families of victims, with criminals and the dispossessed, many of them in the least happy of circumstances. This leads Rebus to see Edinburgh – to my mind one of the best and most beautiful places in the whole world – as a series of crime scenes, and to be always mistrustful of the people he meets. His Edinburgh is not mine.

I have said that I started writing about Edinburgh to make sense of the place. When I was growing up, trips to the capital were few and far between. Maybe it's that my parents just weren't adventurous, or that, never owning a car, the train timetables were against us. I can't recall a single occasion when my father brought us to the city, though my mother managed to show me the Castle and the Museum of Childhood, and would, along with our Aunt Jenny, escort my sister Linda and me to a new film (*Oliver* was one) or Christmas pantomime. Later on, as a teenager at Beath High, I would travel through with friends to prowl the various record shops (including Virgin on Frederick Street), saunter down Rose Street in the mistaken belief that prostitutes might be found there, and head up the always-rakish Cockburn Street towards Greyfriars and Better Books, where S&M 'art' magazines could be browsed. Eventually, towards the end of my school career, we'd be dressed as punks when we made these journeys, seeking out not obscure Van Der Graaf Generator bootlegs but twelve-inch picture-sleeve offerings by the Heartbreakers and the Ramones.

The Edinburgh I arrived in as a student was an extension of this. In my first few terms, I haunted the record shops, and spent Wednesday afternoons (kept free of lectures so that sporting activities could prevail) in a strip bar called Tony's and a soft-core cinema on Nicolson Street. My first term was spent sharing a room with a school friend in a motel on the outskirts of the city. By our second term, we'd found a room in a basement flat facing Bruntsfield Links, and eventually clubbed together with three other school friends to rent a second-floor tenement flat on Morrison Street. These were not glamorous locations, and I was aware that in moving between the various flats and the university, I was seeing layers of Edinburgh and was being introduced to its underbelly. There was a bar near the motel on Peffermill Road. It was called something like the University Arms but was particularly unwelcoming to students. I would tell friends that I'd asked the barman why, being so far from the university, the place merited its name.

'Because if any students come in, we rip their arms off,' came the reply.

He never said any such thing, of course: I made it up, but most of my friends found the story credible. Fiction, after all, can sometimes tell truths the real world can't.

I chose Edinburgh for several reasons. For one thing, most of the kids in my year were going there. For another, the Department of English Literature would allow me to specialise in American Literature (my

North Bridge,
Edinburgh. *He was
remembering all the
suicides he'd dealt with,
people who'd jumped
from North Bridge . . .
It was a crime scene
waiting to happen*
(*The Falls*).

favoured option). Mostly, though, I think I just wanted to be within easy reach of Fife. I didn't know Glasgow, Dundee or Aberdeen at all, St Andrews was too stuffy (Milton was their idea of modern literature), and the thought of applying to universities south of the border never crossed my mind. Edinburgh was the 'safe' option, as well as boasting enough prestige to appease my parents. Their notion of university was that it led to a 'proper' career such as medicine or the law. I wasn't able to tell them how a literature degree could compete with this.

Unlike his creator, Rebus never attended university. In the early books, he has a chip on his shoulder about this, and this chip only grows larger when he finds himself surrounded by younger and younger detectives, the vast majority of whom are college-educated:

Institutes of higher education . . . made him feel stupid. He felt that his every movement, every utterance, was being judged and interpreted, marking him down as a clever man who could have been cleverer, given the breaks   (*Hide and Seek*, p 46).

In interviews I've sometimes said that Rebus represents a way my life could have gone had I not been deemed 'clever' enough for higher education:

In Rebus's youth there had been three obvious career choices for a fifteen-year old boy: the pits, Rosyth Dockyard, or the Army (*The Black Book*, p 127).

I could have added a fourth: the police. I had friends who left school at sixteen or eighteen and joined either the police or one of the armed services. By then, of course, mining was no longer an option. One of my two sisters married an RAF technician, and both of her sons eventually joined up, too. My own father had served in the Durham Light Infantry during World War Two, and I'd lost grandfathers on both sides of the family during World War One. Rebus, too, it is recorded in *Dead Souls*, lost both grandfathers in the course of that conflict. This just about squares with something I learned about Rebus in 1996 or '97, namely that he comes from Polish stock.

Patrolling a
football crowd.

I spent the decade from 1986 away from Edinburgh, living in London for four years and rural France for six. On returning to Edinburgh, I found myself in a bookshop on Dalkeith Road called The Bookworm. Its owner, Peter Ritchie, who has since become a good friend, told me he drank in a pub called Swany's and invited me to join him there some Friday night. This I did, and was introduced to Peter's 'drinking circle', whose members included a gentleman by the name of Joe Rebus. Having startled me further by telling he lived on a street called Rankin Drive, Joe proceeded to explain that the family name was Polish. I decided that night that Rebus would have Polish roots, too. After all, growing up in Fife, a good number of my classmates had sported East European-sounding surnames. There had been economic migrations to Scotland in the late-nineteenth and early-twentieth centuries, to take advantage of employment opportunities in heavy engineering and traditional industries such as coal. It seems to me feasible that Rebus's father's father could have come to Scotland, found a wife, and sired Rebus's father before heading off to fight for his new homeland in the trenches.

All of this led me to the eventual writing of *Fleshmarket Close*, in which Rebus has to deal with asylum seekers (genuine and otherwise) and the new market in illegal economic migrants. Scotland used to pride itself on having a welcome ready for visitors and the dispossessed. We saw ourselves as reaching out to Europe and Scandinavia (necessary for trade at one time, whenever we were in conflict with England). We sent our sons and daughters overseas to launch themselves on new continents, stretching from Nova Scotia to the southern tip of New Zealand. At the same time, we were a mongrel nation, pillaged and settled in turn by a variety of cultures, from Norse and Celtic to Anglo Saxon. It sometimes seemed to us (lazily, in retrospect) that we were far too busy with religious bigotry to have any time for racism. Certainly, those kids with the East European names were made welcome – they were Scots, after all, and they were white (and Protestant). I'm not sure a Catholic kid could have walked with so blithe a heart into my school playground:

'What in Christ's name is happening here?' he found himself asking.
The world passed by, determined not to notice: cars grinding

> homewards; pedestrians making eye contact only with the pavement
> ahead of them, because what you didn't see couldn't hurt you. A fine,
> brave world awaiting the new parliament. An ageing country,
> dispatching its talents to the four corners of the globe . . .
> unwelcoming to visitor and migrant alike   (*Fleshmarket Close*, p 170).

If my original project had been a greater understanding of the city of Edinburgh, those parameters soon changed, once I'd discovered that Rebus was a tough enough creation to lead the reader into an investigation of Scotland itself: a small, proud and ancient country with a confused and fragile sense of its own identity. This is the landscape I inherited, with Detective Inspector John Rebus as my guide. As a nation, Scotland has been called 'the arse of Europe' (by a Papal Legate in 1529) and a place of immense civilisation (by Voltaire, no less). Betjeman and Walpole have sung the praises of Edinburgh, while others (including some of its most famed citizens) have decried the suffocating petty-mindedness of the place. A contradictory city makes a good capital for a country of contradictions. Growing up in Scotland, I was only ever aware of my Scottishness when our national team were playing football, or some sporting legend was winning gold, or when we ventured south of the border to places where my accent proved a challenge. At university, I studied *English* rather than Scottish Literature (the latter being available only as a one-year supplementary course at that time), and wasn't aware of Scottish writing of any contemporary vibrancy until Alasdair Gray's *Lanark* came along – at just the right time for me. *Lanark* was a teeming, confident novel about Scotland past, present and future, and came as a welcome respite from books which seemed always to be looking over their shoulder to historical mistakes and grievances. Suddenly readers were turning to the urban experience of Glasgow for insights into the world, and writers such as Gray, James Kelman and William McIlvanney were happy to oblige.

While in Edinburgh, of course, we had *The Prime of Miss Jean Brodie*, published as far back as 1961 and set in the distant 1930s. With that book, Muriel Spark had defined Edinburgh for a generation. But that landscape would soon change.

2

Who is Rebus?

I TOOK THE DECISION early on in the series that John Rebus would live in 'real time'. That is to say, he would age between books. After all, if I wanted to write about the changing face of Scotland, it was more realistic if my detective was allowed to change, too. Rebus is affected by every case he works on, and carries with him the ghosts of every victim. Police officers have often commented that he feels real to them, and the Chief Constable of Lothian and Borders Police went so far as to state that he wished he had one officer like Rebus on the force – high praise, as far as I was concerned.

I never did spend too much time fretting over Rebus's chronology, and it's down to luck rather than planning that the facts of his life remain consistent (more or less) over the course of the series – though I've been fortunate in later years that a fan has compiled a database for me, including a Rebus 'time-line'. Rebus was born just after World War Two and, in the early 1960s (aged fifteen) joined the Army (from a sense of guilty duty rather than any real passion). He eventually joined the Parachute Regiment, and was in Northern Ireland early on in 'the Troubles'. An incident there made him want to get out, and he opted to train for the SAS. That training broke him, and he was allowed to leave the Army on medical grounds. He recuperated in the East Neuk of Fife, where eventually he would meet and marry Rhona. And at some point, he joined the City of Edinburgh Police (now defunct). By the time we first meet him, he has been a cop for the best part of fifteen years.

By now, a further eighteen years into the series, Rebus has spent over half his life living and working in Edinburgh, yet he remains a Fifer at heart, as does his creator. I lived in Fife for eighteen of my forty-five years, and seldom return, yet I remain a Fifer 'by formation' (as Muriel Spark might put it), and this is reflected in my use of Fife in the Rebus novels. In practically every book there is mention of Fife, or the use of some memory from my time there. Our first glimpse of Rebus is as he visits his father's grave in Cardenden. Immediately afterwards, he heads for 'the skull-grey coast' and Kirkcaldy. I seem to have had some issues about my birthplace in *Knots and Crosses*, and would never afterwards be so cynical about Fife. Three books into the series, Rebus is reminiscing about his time as a grocer's 'message-boy', making deliveries on a heavy-framed bicycle. This takes me back to the grocer's in Lochgelly where my father worked. As a kid, I would sometimes spend time there, though I was never his message-boy (I was too young, the bike too heavy for me). In *The Falls* Rebus remembers his father telling him a story about walking into a grocer's (in Lochgelly) on a bitter winter's morning and asking the manager 'Is that your Ayrshire bacon?' to which the manager, warming himself by the fire, replies 'No, it's my hands I'm heating'. (Arse-you're-baking . . . no, never mind.) This was a story told to me many times by my own father, who swore it had really happened. Maybe for a while, I even believed him.

There were few books in the home where I grew up, but from an early age I was keen on stories. As a young child, I'd slip into bed between my parents on a Sunday morning and my dad would regale me with tales about a recurring character called Johnny Morey, making up the scenes as he went along. Johnny's adventures took place in Bowhill itself, and years afterwards I realised that my dad was extrapolating from his own childhood adventures. In other words, he was doing what all writers do: mining his experiences for fiction, reshaping those memories into a narrative with a pleasing structure. (I once talked about Johnny Morey during a book-signing event and a woman from the west coast of Scotland came up to me to say that her father, too, spoke of Johnny Morey. It seems he is part of a wider folk tradition than I had realised.)

As a kid, I sought out stories of all kinds. Almost every day, there was a new comic I wanted to buy at the local newsagent, moving seamlessly from the *Bimbo* to the *Beano* and *Dandy* and from there to the *Victor, Hotspur* and *Lion and Tiger*. Then there were all the Gerry Anderson tie-ins, comics such as *TV21*. My favourite Christmas presents were annuals, which I would read a dozen or more times apiece. When out playing, I'd most likely be planning all-out war or pretending that

I was protecting Bowhill from alien attack. I made my own comics, too, by folding plain pieces of paper in half, drawing separate stories on each page (and adding free gifts such as home-made badges to the cover as an incentive).

Eventually, the town's library became my second home. It had been built with subscriptions from the town's mining community (as had the swimming-pool next door). It opened another world to me, letting me access 'adult' books such as *The Godfather* and *Shaft*. As I entered my teens, I started writing poems, song lyrics and short stories. One diary entry from 1975 even records an attempted novel entitled *Armageddon*. I was using my pocket money to buy books by Frederick Forsyth and Alistair MacLean (himself Scottish and a Gaelic speaker, though I didn't know it then), and was watching TV programmes about books (usually fronted by a youthful Melvyn Bragg). I would buy just about anything these programmes recommended, which is why I ended up slogging my way through *The Gulag Archipelago Volume 2* and being seduced by Ian McEwan's first collection of short stories. McEwan appealed to me particularly because he seemed to find erotic potential in the most mundane settings – something bound to appeal to a teenager living in a fairly unexciting town.

It seems to me now that back then I was living most of my life in an alternative reality, one existing only in my head. Where this passion for the fictive came from I can only speculate. Maybe it had something to do with Bowhill itself. As an infant, I'd been aware of a klaxon sounding three times a day, indicating a change of shifts at the pit. Miners would head off to work in their pristine work-clothes, carrying a 'piece-box' containing thick-cut sandwiches and a flask of tea, and return home at the next klaxon blackened and exhausted. My own father had been unusual in not heading for a job in the pits (my grandmother, wary of the injuries and illnesses she saw around her, forbid it). But I had uncles and cousins who worked the mines, up until the day those mines were declared uneconomic. Suddenly, while not yet a teenager, I became aware that the klaxon had stopped sounding. Families were moving to other areas where mines still operated. Middle-aged men were opting for re-training (often for non-existent jobs). Many people settled for the dole.

PERSEVERE COURT

Unseen, a little bit of life seemed to seep out of my home town. The place was as resilient as ever – on the surface. But surface was what it was. The brave face predominated, because anything else would have signified weakness and capitulation. Several times in my books Rebus is described as being 'thrawn', meaning stubborn:

Persevere Court in Edinburgh. The sentiment seems ready-made for Cardenden.

The Scots tended to crack jokes with a straight face and be deadly serious when they smiled   (*Mortal Causes*, p 42);

She never knew when he was being serious. People in Edinburgh were like that: obtuse, thrawn. Sometimes she thought he was flirting, that the jibes and jokes were part of some mating ritual made all the more complex because it consisted of baiting the subject rather than wooing them   (*Set In Darkness*, p 173).

In both cases we are sharing the thoughts of Siobhan Clarke. Siobhan is a handy commentator in that she, too, is an outsider, born of English parents and boasting an English accent. This is almost certainly why, having entered the series as just another of Rebus's colleagues at St Leonard's, she soon usurped Rebus's regular sidekick (Brian Holmes) and began carving out her own territory. College-educated, left-leaning, and much younger than Rebus, she could almost be said to represent the author. Siobhan sees traits in Rebus and the Scots in general that many of us might not see in ourselves. As a race, the Scots tend towards reticence, something outsiders find curious. They expect us to be as garrulous and outward-looking as the Irish – we're all Celts beneath the skin, after all. But if Ireland is the Celtic Tigger, bouncing around all over the place, then Scotland is more like Eeyore, unsure of itself and staying quiet until it knows it is safe to speak. '"Behold the Scottish male, at his happiest when in denial",' is how one character puts it in *The Hanging Garden*, while Rebus himself seems to acknowledge the problem while out walking in St Andrews:

The promenade was empty, save for a Labrador being walked by its owner. As the man passed them, he smiled, bowed his head. A typically Scots greeting: more evasion than anything else (*Set In Darkness*, pp 188–9).

Typically Scots . . . more evasion
than anything else.

RIGHT: A hail-shower, Edinburgh.

Such reticence, of course, is a strength in some areas. The Scots are seen as being 'canny' in business matters, which is why our economy remains strong in invisibles such as banking and insurance. 'Invisibles' is an interesting term in itself. The journalist James Campbell wrote a book called *Invisible Country*, detailing his attempt to travel around and define Scotland. Others have tried before and since, most notably Edwin Muir. Yet somehow a clear notion of the Scots and Scottishness remains out of reach. Charles McKean, in his book *Edinburgh*, says of the city-dwellers that 'their response to war and invasion was to make themselves invisible (by hiding in tunnels beneath the Castle and the Old Town); and in due course that habit, born of necessity, became endemic in the Edinburgh character'. McKean also speaks of Enlightenment Edinburgh and how it made 'an aristocracy of aptitude'. It is certainly true that in the past, Scotland was famed for its 'democratic intellect', the idea that we are measured not by outward show but by inner qualities. The Scots abhor pretension and bragging. The problem with this, of course, is that it tends to stifle novelty, creativity, difference, new thinking and intellectualism. We're all supposed to be cut from the same cloth – 'all Jock Tamson's bairns', as the Scots saying goes – and not supposed to act differently from our fellows. This reticence extends to the entire UK in some issues. For example, the American academic Arthur Herman wrote a book which, in the USA, was published as *How the Scots Invented the Modern World*. The subtitle of this book was *The True Story of How Western Europe's Poorest Nation Created Our World and Everything In It*. To be sure, there is some hyperbole here, but Herman argues his case fluently. However, when his book was published in the UK, it was re-titled *The Scottish Enlightenment*. You had to look at the subtitle (*The Scots' Invention of the Modern World*) to find even a hint of saltire-waving – and that subtitle was given on the jacket in much smaller lettering, just to be on the safe side. After all, it wouldn't do to offend . . .

Can any of the blame for this be attributed to the figure of Protestant reformer John Knox? In the sixteenth century he and his followers made sure it was difficult for the Scots to do anything frivolous or pleasurable: carnivals and mumming were banned, while blasphemers and adulterers could be tortured and hanged. Doom was a certainty in any case, gently mocked by poet Alastair Reid in his poem 'Scotland' with its closing refrain: 'We'll pay for it, we'll pay for it, we'll pay for it'. Is it any wonder that when the Edinburgh-born mathematician John Napier invented logarithms (less than half a century after Knox's death) he did so not merely in order to bamboozle generations of school-children but actually to calculate the date of the Apocalypse?

(1738, by the way.)

A character in *Dead Souls* puts it like this:

'We're just not supposed to have it all, are we? We're supposed to fail gloriously. Anything we succeed at, we keep low-profile. It's our failures we're allowed to trumpet.'

Rebus smiled. 'Might be something in that.'

'It runs right through our history.'

'And ends at the national football team.'

Rebus, throughout the books, remains a product of his environment, hardly helped by the career he has chosen. Cops cannot go home at night and discuss with impunity at the dinner-table their day's quota of assaults, overdoses and misery. As a result, they bottle things up, or hang around with empathetic souls – meaning other cops. The force comes to supplant their family, and it takes a strong relationship to survive:

Rebus had always found relationships with the opposite sex difficult. He'd grown up in a mining village, a bit behind the times when it came to things like promiscuity. You stuck your hand in a girl's blouse and next thing her father was after you with a leather belt.

Then he'd joined the army, where women were by turns fantasy figures and untouchables: slags and madonnas, there seemed no middle ground. Released from the army, he'd joined the police. Married by then, but his job had proved more seductive, more all-consuming than the relationship – than *any* relationship   (*Black and Blue*, pp 189-90)

It seemed to me from the start that a Scottish Presbyterian cop would have it harder than most. When his mentor dies in *Black and Blue*, Rebus still finds a display of emotion impossible:

LEFT: George IV Bridge
from the Cowgate.

ABOVE: Marchmont by moonlight.

Typical Scot, he couldn't cry about it. Crying was for football defeats, animal bravery stories. *Flower of Scotland* after closing time. He cried about stupid things, but tonight his eyes remained stubbornly dry.

His sometime lover Patience, however, sees another aspect of his character when she says that he likes to 'antagonise just to get a response', adding that 'conflict is more *fun* for you than consensus' (*Let It Bleed*). Rebus's defence that he's just playing devil's advocate strikes her as lame. Patience returns to the fray later on in the same book, when dispensing afternoon tea to Rebus and his daughter Sammy:

'You see, Sammy, your father is the Old Testament type: retribution rather than rehabilitation . . . And he's the classic Calvinist, too. Let the punishment fit the crime, and then some.'
    'That's not Calvinism,' Rebus said. 'It's Gilbert and Sullivan.'

Another classic Scottish ploy: retreating into humour when a situation starts to become uncomfortably serious. It's a tactic Rebus even uses with his bosses, but his Chief Constable is wise to him:

'It's a good act,' he commented, 'but then you've spent years perfecting it, haven't you?'
    'What act is that, sir?'
    'The wisecracks; that hint of insubordination. Your way of coping with a situation until you've had a chance to digest it'
(*Resurrection Men*, p 89).

When people ask me how I know what it's like to be a cop like Rebus, I'm apt to shrug. There's no clear answer, except to say that writers are usually good at empathising with a whole variety of character-types. I know what it's like to be obsessed: I'm an obsessive myself. I have worked in various agencies, organisations and offices where politicking and careerism were rife. I couldn't see that the police force would be much different from the civil service or journalism. I was never happy in these environments, trusting my own instincts over the orders of my superiors. At the same time, it seems to me that the figures of the

detective and the novelist are similar in some ways. Both seek the truth, through creating a narrative from apparently chaotic or unconnected events. Both are interested in human nature and motivation. Both are voyeurs. (The Edinburgh-born Muriel Spark says that she and her fellow novelists 'loiter with intent' – playing on the idea of a criminal activity.) I certainly enjoy dipping into other people's lives, giving fresh texture and tone to them, while Rebus has his own reasons for prying into everyone else's secrets:

> His work sustained him only because it was an easy option. He dealt every day with strangers, with people who didn't mean anything to him in the wider scheme. He could enter their lives, and leave again just as easily. He got to live other people's lives, or at least portions of them, experiencing things at one remove, which wasn't nearly as challenging as the real thing . . . And if he became obsessed with his case-work, well, that was no different from being obsessed with train numbers or cigarette cards or rock albums. Obsession came easy – especially to men – because it was a cheap way of achieving *control* (*Hanging Garden*, p 372).

By the time of *The Falls*, Rebus can put it more succinctly: 'He concentrated on the minutiae of other people's lives, other people's problems, to stop him examining his own frailties and failings'. His colleagues worry about his obsession with work. Fellow DI Jack Morton thinks Rebus 'a loner even in company, his brain and heart only fully engaged when he was working a case' and worries that his tenacity could also be a weakness, 'blinding him to danger, making him impatient and reckless', while Siobhan Clarke goes an intriguing stage further:

> She worried that he relished the idea of his own fallibility. He was only human, and if proving it meant enduring pain and defeat, he would welcome both. Did that mean he had a martyr complex? (*Resurrection Men*, p 392).

It does sometimes seem to me that the Scots suffer from something more complex than an inferiority complex. It's almost as if we *enjoy* failure, embracing it with masochistic zeal. Again, this may go back to the pull of 'democracy', to 'tall poppy syndrome'. Our few stars, be they in the fields of entertainment, the arts, or elsewhere, must always be down to earth, for fear of being sneered at. When Billy Connolly plays laird of the manor with his Hollywood pals, Scots are liable to laugh at him rather than with him.

Change, too, is frowned upon in many quarters, as has always been the case. Lord Cockburn, one-time Provost of Edinburgh, comments in his diaries of the early 1800s that the moving of the city's fish market to a more hygienic setting provoked outcry on the grounds of 'tradition'. Over half a century later, in his book *Picturesque Notes*, Robert Louis Stevenson criticises new building projects such as the 'villas' which were then being constructed in areas such as Morningside and Newington (the same houses which are today among Edinburgh's most expensive and sought-after). Tensions remain in the current century. The new Scottish Parliament complex has roused easily as many detractors as champions, while any attempts to introduce radical new designs to Edinburgh are sure to be stymied and opposed.

Rebus, I feel sure, is conservative in these matters. The status quo suits him fine in many ways. In this aspect, as in a multitude of others, he and I differ. He comes from a slightly older generation (albeit the generation which gave the world Hendrix and Dylan), and is less the liberal than I am. When I start writing a book, I know I am about to enter a debate with the creature I am bringing back to life. My attitudes will not necessarily be his. In *Dead Souls*, for example, he shares the same knee-jerk reaction towards paedophiles as many Britons, then feels slightly ashamed by his consequent actions, actions which lead to a murder. In *Hanging Garden* he has to think long and hard about the necessity of punishing old men for their actions in a war from half a century back. In *Fleshmarket Close* I drop the political hot potato of immigration into his lap.

Why? To challenge him, and perhaps to challenge my own assertions and beliefs, too. As I say, the books always feel like a debate, sometimes with a concrete answer at the end, but oftentimes not. Does this bring me any closer to explaining who Rebus is? I'm doubtful. The reason I continue to write about him is because I still don't feel I know every-

thing there is to know about him. In some ways he's a typical working-class Scottish male, happiest with his music, his junk food, and the drinkers at his favoured pub. But there are layers to his personality, and many of these layers stay hidden, in the grand Scots tradition. The community he grew up in made him resilient and reticent. The city he lives in shapes his attitudes and philosophy of life. The job he does provides him with thorny questions to which he seeks often uncomfortable answers. Like his creator, Rebus is trying to make sense of the world around him. His quests become the reader's, so that we're all made to share his quandaries, whether or not we also share his get-out clauses: the booze, the smokes, the music.

It's fortunate I'll never meet him: I have the feeling we wouldn't get along . . .

Inside St Leonard's.

OPPOSITE: Outside St Leonard's.

LEFT: The Scottish Parliament.

BELOW: The Union Canal, Edinburgh.

3

Church and State

FOR CENTURIES NOW, religion in Scotland has been a messy business. In Edinburgh's Greyfriars Kirkyard a monument lists the many seceders and reformers who were condemned for their beliefs. Until our new parliament building was completed, MSPs met at the Church of Scotland HQ at the top of The Mound in Edinburgh, passing a louring statue of John Knox as they walked indoors. (Knox was not known for his mild-mannered views on women and Catholics. Arthur Herman calls the Ulster Scots 'genuine legatees of John Knox, with their fundamentalist religious zeal, their aggressive egalitarianism, and "their love of education and their anxiety to have an educated ministry"'). Beyond the monuments and traditions, however, lie bitter allegiances which bleed into the present. I still remember how, as a three- and four-year old, I played regularly with a kid across the street from me. His name was Miles and he was a Catholic. Not that I knew this at the time. However, different schools awaited us when we reached the age of five, and in those schools we made different friends, eventually drifting apart into what seems to me now a curious, unspoken apartheid. In Scotland, no one needs to ask 'Are you a Prod or a Pape?' Instead, they'll sift evidence such as your Christian name and surname, or your football allegiance, to glean all the information they need.

During those childhood years of mine, I would be wakened from my sleep just after closing-time each Saturday night by drunken singing of 'The Sash My Father Wore', an anti-Catholic lyric gifted us by the Irish Troubles. I would climb from my bed and peer through the curtains towards the other end of the cul-de-sac. A couple of Catholic families lived there, which might explain why the singer (the same man every week?) paused in his homewards stagger to offer up the full force of his tunelessness.

No one ever dared outside to remonstrate.

During the football season buses would pull up outside the Rex Cinema to take the faithful to Glasgow. Only ever Rangers fans, I seem to remember – not many Catholics in Cardenden, even if the town's most famous

John Knox at work.

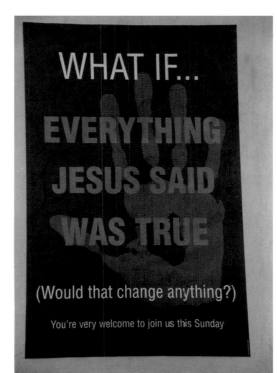

footballing son, Johnny Thomson, had played for Celtic. (He was killed during an 'Old Firm' game when a Rangers player accidentally kicked him in the head.) And in the summer, when the football was on hold, the marching season began: Orange banners, flutes, drums sounding like heartbeats. White-gloved elders, their faces reddened with drink. One night, as a teenager, I was supping at the Bowhill Hotel when a friend suggested we go upstairs to where the day's festivities were concluding. The young men were still playing their flutes, shirts clinging with sweat. Plenty of noise, I thought, but little substance. And then it was time for the National Anthem, but one young drinker refused to rise to his feet. I marvelled at his stubborn bravery – even I wasn't that reckless; I was standing up, just like the others. In *Mortal Causes*, I gave this experience to Rebus:

Forth Rail Bridge, umbilical cord between Fife and Edinburgh.

> There'd been an Orange march in Cowdenbeath. The pub they were in seemed to be hosting a crowd of the marchers in the dance hall upstairs. Sounds of drums, especially the huge drum they called the *lambeg*, and flutes and penny whistles... They'd gone upstairs to investigate, just as the thing was winding down. *God Save the Queen* was being destroyed on a dozen cheap flutes.
>
> And some of the kids singing along, sweaty brows and shirts open, some of them had their arms raised, hands straight out in front of them . . .

A few years before, I'd been riveted by a TV play set in Glasgow during a Loyalist parade. *Just Another Saturday*, it was called, with Billy Connolly starring in his first non-comic role. The ugliness and veracity of the casual violence stayed long in my memory, but I wouldn't feel able to write about this aspect of my upbringing until *Mortal Causes*, six novels into the Rebus series, and when I did, some Protestants weren't happy that I'd made 'them' the villains of the piece, rather than concentrating on the Republicans. One letter-writer told me it might have been fitting if I'd died at the hands of an IRA bomb . . .

The Church I'd been born into was a world away from the Troubles: Sunday School picnics on the links at Burntisland, the hired coaches strewn with streamers; a packet of mints to while away the sermon; Scripture Union meetings on the beach at St Andrews during our summer holiday there. On the day the old and much-loved minister at St Fothad's was due to retire, there was spontaneous applause in church, something he chastised us for, but gently. His replacement was cut from more progressive cloth – even sporting a beard – and I could tell my mother wasn't impressed. This didn't deter the new minister from making regular and unannounced home visits, which entailed the dusting-off of the good tea-service and much 'off-stage' whispering. As Rebus himself puts it in *Let It Bleed*, 'ministers didn't make friends, not easily; they were like cops that way. People were always afraid they'd say the wrong thing in front of them.'

If I had to describe my family, I'd say we were timid. We had 'rich' relations in the next town over – rich in that they owned things like cars and their own homes, while my parents did not – and trips to see them were fraught. We were always fearful of some faux pas, and this extended to our church-going. Just before the start of one service, my sister accidentally upturned a bag of pan-drops. They landed noisily on the wooden floor and started rolling down the ranks of pews, the congregation stooping to capture them and hand them back. She was hellish embarrassed, and remained so for years afterwards.

I stopped going to church eventually. The way I remember it, my mother came to me when I was twelve or thirteen and said something like 'You're old enough to decide for yourself – you can keep coming to church with your sister and me, or stay home like your dad'. The thing was, I had become a chameleon, appearing to fit in with the kids around me. During the walk to church and back, I was self-conscious, knowing that the gang who hung around at the street-corner would be staring. I would be standing out from their crowd, and I didn't want that. It was hard enough as it was to look like I fitted in. If they started seeing me as 'different', they might eventually find out that I was writing poems, stories and song lyrics in my spare time. So I stayed home on Sundays, and went to church only to attend weddings, christenings and funerals. In my short story 'Sunday' (published in *A Good Hanging and Other Stories*) I give this memory to Rebus:

Soon the church bells would start ringing, calling the faithful. Rebus would not answer. He had given up church-going. Any day but

Sunday he might have gone. But Sunday, Sunday was the only day off he had. He remembered his mother, taking him with her to church every Sunday while his father stayed at home in bed with tea and the paper. Then one Sunday . . . his mother had said he could choose . . .

For me, disillusionment had set in the previous Christmas. We always attended the service late on Christmas Eve, but this one time some drunken teenagers – boys I recognised from a few years above me at school – squeezed into the pew in front of ours and started making fun of the whole thing, snuffing out the candles on the ledge next to them, snorting and belching. No one told them to stop; we all pretended we could neither see nor hear them. One of their number, I recall, had spray-painted his bovver boots silver. Maybe this gang were the ones behind the rise in graffiti all over Cardenden. Someone had even painted the words REMEMBER 1690 on the main road. 1690: the Battle of the Boyne, won by William of Orange – King Billy to his disciples. Even aged twelve, I'd wondered at the dauber's stupidity: within days, the message would have been erased by the daily weight of vehicles passing over it.

 Here before me in church on Christmas Eve was the world of *A Clockwork Orange* made flesh. The congregation suddenly seemed puny and violated, and I could see no further sense in it.

From the start of the Rebus series, my detective was a troubled man, seeking answers to big questions. He would attend a range of churches, investigate a number of faiths. In *Strip Jack* he calls himself 'a kind of Christian' who was raised as a 'Pessimisterian' – in other words, a Presbyterian pessimist. And in *Tooth and Nail* we find the following:

He's asking for trouble doing this. He's *begging* for it, like a black-clothed Calvinist pleading to be beaten for his sins. A lash across the back. Rebus had seen them all, all the available religions. He had tasted them and each one tasted bitter in its own particular way. Where was the religion for those who did not feel guilty, did not feel shame, did not regret getting angry or getting even or, better yet, getting more than even? Where was the religion for a man who believed that good and bad must coexist, even within the individual? Where was the religion for a man who believed in God but not in God's religion?

There's cynicism here, but also longing on the part of Rebus: he's desperate for answers to the questions he poses. Later on in the series, he would get to spend evenings in conversation with a priest, Father Conor Leary, the two men busy in debate as they sip their Guinness and whisky. Leary is introduced (in voice only – Rebus is in the confessional) in *The Black Book*, and tells Rebus to come and talk to him again: "'I like to know what madness you Prods are thinking. It gives me something to chew on when there's nothing good on the telly.'" The introduction of the priest paves the way for the paramilitary storyline in *Mortal Causes*. It's a curious coincidence that several years after the book was published, a drug gang which claimed to have links to the Ulster Volunteer Force tried to muscle its way into an Edinburgh housing-scheme. At the time I wrote it, the story was fiction; later on it came at least partially true.

As a young man, we learn in *Mortal Causes*, Rebus himself went on an Orange Lodge march. Here he is describing a contemporary march through Edinburgh city centre:

All these semi-inebriated working men and retired men, quiet family types who might belong to the British Legion or their local Ex-Servicemen's Club, who might inhabit the bowling green on summer evenings and go with their families on holiday to Spain or Florida or Largs. It was only when you saw them in groups like this that you caught a whiff of something else. Alone, they had nothing but a nagging complaint; together, they had a voice: the sound of the *lambeg*, dense as a heartbeat; the insistent flutes; the march. They always fascinated Rebus. He couldn't help it. It was in his blood. He'd marched in his youth. He'd done a lot of things back then.

By the time of *Mortal Causes*, Rebus has grown wiser:

Scotland had enough problems without getting involved in Ireland's. They were like Siamese twins who'd refused the operation to separate them. Only one twin had been forced into a marriage with England, and the other was hooked on self-mutilation. They didn't need politicians to sort things out; they needed a psychiatrist.

The marching season, the season of the Protestant, was over for another year, give or take the occasional fringe procession. Now it was the season of the International Festival, a festive time, a time to forget the small and insecure country you lived in.

Time indeed.

Recently in Scotland politicians have been arguing that it's time to put an end to sectarianism once and for all. Usually these sentiments appear in the wake of another Rangers-Celtic match, with its attendant violence and hatred (on the part of the so-called 'supporters' of either team). But then someone will write to the newspapers to stress that sectarianism is a problem specific to Glasgow. In football terms, this is largely true: largely, but not wholly. In *Resurrection Men*, Rebus is given a tour of Glasgow by hard-bitten fellow detective Francis Gray:

Barras Market, Glasgow.

> In Bridgeton, they passed the ground of Celtic FC: Parkhead to civilians like Rebus; Paradise to the club's supporters.
> 'This'll be the Catholic end of town then,' Rebus commented.
> He knew that the Rangers stadium – Ibrox – was practically next door to Govan, where Gray was stationed. So he added: 'And you'll be a blue-nose?'
> 'I support Rangers,' Gray agreed. 'Have done all my life. Are you a Hearts man?'
> 'I'm not really anything.'
> Gray looked at him. 'You must be something.'
> 'I don't go to games.'
> 'What about when you watch on TV?' Rebus just shrugged.
> 'I mean, there's only two teams playing at any one time . . . you must take *sides*?'
> 'Not really.'
> 'Say it was Rangers against Celtic . . .' Gray was growing annoyed. 'You're a Protestant, right?'
> 'What's that got to do with it?'
> 'Well, Christ's sake, man, you'd be on Rangers' side, wouldn't you?'
> 'I don't know, they've never asked me to play.'
> Gray let out a snort of frustration.

'See', Rebus went on, 'I didn't realise it was meant to be religious warfare . . .'

He does realise it, of course, but enjoys winding up Gray, who is another instance of the 'Clockwork Orangeman' found in the early books. Is the desegregation of schooling an answer to Scotland's sectarian divide? Probably not, though it would be a start, so that kids like me could continue to play with kids like Miles. What's really needed though is an end not only to the conflict in Northern Ireland but to the pockets of sheer loathing which can be found on either side of the barricade, a loathing borne of tradition, handed down the generations and thereby difficult to eradicate. If the erroneous anger and mistrust are to disappear, it will take generations, too, the changes incremental and almost invisible to the eye. Rebus, it has to be said, is less hopeful than his creator.

In part this is because he himself does not trust politicians to do the job. If the history of religion in Scotland is messy, then politics needs a radiation suit. I grew up in an apolitical household. My parents never discussed politics. They would leave together for the polling station, my mother probably to vote Conservative, my father Labour. When I was thirteen, a new teacher of English arrived at Auchterderran Junior High. He was active in the Scottish National Party (in fact, I think he was a councillor in nearby Kirkcaldy). He was young and humorous and had long hair. The kids fell for him. When another general election loomed, he supervised a mock version in the school, cannily enlisting a charming hardman as SNP candidate. The result was a landslide. (Later on, this same teacher branched out into fashion. I bought a shiny purple mod suit from his shop in Kirkcaldy.) This was the early 1970s, and there was a whiff of revolt in the air. One day at school – I forget why – we all decided to go on strike, burning work-books and the occasional school tie. There may even have been a mini-rampage through the school. Certainly there was mass truancy, with many of us repairing to the local snooker hall, which is where we were found by the police. The status quo resumed soon afterwards, with the ring-leaders probably being rewarded with a few whacks of the leather belt known as either the 'tawse' or 'the Lochgelly' (this latter being its place of manufacture, and the next town along from Cardenden: nice to see traditional, local industries being supported). When I got the belt it was usually for not shutting up or for truancy. It didn't happen often: I'd learned the art of camouflage, blending in with my surroundings. Despite this, there were a few incidents at my Junior High. In one, I was thrown into a thorn-bush, presumably for 'being different'. Maybe I wasn't such a great chameleon after all. It took days with a pair of tweezers to remove the last of the tiny barbs.

When I was deemed clever enough to move to the Senior High (at the end of my second year), it came as some relief. There, I would meet kids with the same interests as me – music and books. Pranks, of course, were still permissible. The part of Fife where I grew up had always been a left-wing heartland. A state of UDI had been declared during the General Strike (my Aunt Jenny rebelling against this by cycling along the railway line to fetch deliveries of newspapers from the station at Cowdenbeath to her parents' shop in Lochgelly). Fife had sent the first Communist MP to the London parliament in 1935 – his name was Willie Gallacher, a founder of the British Communist Party, and he was MP for Fife West until 1950 – and still, in the 1970s, could boast old-style Communists on some of its councils. There was one man in particular who wrote letters to the weekly *Central Fife Times*, bemoaning the lack of any Stalinist backbone to the country. So a few of us sat down one day and typed a letter of our own, claiming to represent the Fascist Party of Beath High School. The resulting backlash was predictable, as was the hunt by the headmaster to find the culprits. Best of all, however, as far as we jokers were concerned, was that at least one letter of wholehearted support for our spurious group appeared in the paper the following week.

That stunt remained my only involvement in politics for quite some time. Even now, I'm apt to float. When the producers of BBC1's 'Question Time' invited me on to their programme, they had an interviewer ask me for all manner of opinions, in an effort to pin down my politics – they failed, finding me to the right on some issues, the left on others, and the middle on everything else. Rebus, on the other hand . . . well, I'm not sure. I would surmise that most real-life police officers would lean to the right. But Rebus tells us in *Strip Jack* that he's only voted three

times in his life: 'Once Labour, once SNP, and once Tory'. That book represented my first use of Scottish politics as both theme and plot, its intent signalled by the original jacket design (the first and last time I had creative input into what appears on my covers). The hardcover edition of *Strip Jack* showed a Lion Rampant flying over the Houses of Parliament. I thought it nicely cheeky at the time, as Scotland was still debating devolution. After going on to use 'the Troubles' as the backdrop to *Mortal Causes*, I then shifted emphasis to local politics in *Let It Bleed*, and by the time of *Set In Darkness* we learn that political differences with his wife led (at least in part) to the eventual break-up of Rebus's marriage:

Queensberry House, home to both the Scottish Parliament and an act of cannibalism.

March 1, 1979. The referendum had a clause attached. Forty percent of the electorate had to vote Yes. The rumour was, the Labour government down in London wanted obstacles put in the way of devolution. They feared that Scottish Westminster MPs would be lost, and that the Conservatives would be gifted a permanent majority in the Commons. Forty percent had to vote Yes.

It wasn't even close. Thirty-three said Yes, thirty-one No. The turnout was just under sixty-four percent. The result, as one paper put it, was 'a nation divided'. The SNP withdrew their support for the Callaghan government – he called them 'turkeys voting for Christmas' – an election had to be called, and the Conservatives came back into power, led by Margaret Thatcher.

'Your SNP did that', Rebus told Rhona. 'Now where's your devolution?'

She just shrugged a response, beyond goading. They'd come a long way since the cushion-fights on the floor. He turned to his work instead, immersing himself in other people's lives, other people's problems and miseries.

And hadn't voted in an election since.

Nor did he vote in the devolution referendum: his ultimate revenge against Rhona.

Devolution did eventually come, of course, the new parliament providing me with material for *Set In Darkness*. That novel was reviewed

Industrious Scotland (Grangemouth Oil Refinery).

on BBC radio by our then First Minister Donald Dewar. He found the book not to his taste, but was also impressed by the level of behind-the-scenes detail. When he died, his library became part of the new Scottish Parliament complex at the foot of the Canongate, and *Set In Darkness* became the only work of contemporary Scottish fiction in the parliament library.

When it comes to elections, the Scots are apt to think with their hearts but vote with their heads. We're also fast to take offence and can be hyper-critical. As Robert Louis Stevenson put it in his essay *Picturesque Notes*, we are 'wonderful patient haters for conscience sake up here in the North'. This strikes me as true. Feuds and grudges can last down the ages. At my own father's funeral, there was a (short-lived) falling-out over who should and should not have been invited to the sit-down meal after the burial. I used this in *The Black Book*, but swapping the funeral for a wedding in a piece of secret family history revealed to Rebus by his aunt in Aberdeen. In the 1960s, people in Cardenden would cross the street to avoid the kin of a 'scab' from the days of the General Strike. If any Fifers scabbed during the 1984 miners' strike, I'm sure the same treatment awaited them, and may be meted out upon their children and grandchildren, too.

Wonderful patient haters indeed.

The chronology of the Rebus novels straddles industrial and post-industrial Scotland, which is why I write at length about new technologies (in *Let It Bleed*), oil (in *Black and Blue*) and coal (whenever Rebus returns to his native Fife). Rebus was born into a Scotland reliant on traditional industries and heavy engineering. As those industries collapsed in the 1960s and '70s, the sense of despair grew. Many communities felt they only existed to serve the local industry. Cardenden, for example, had been a hamlet and some farms until King Coal arrived, bringing a workforce with it (including my own family – from the established coalfields of Lanarkshire – and probably Rebus's too). Scotland's identity was linked inextricably to work. With the demise of one, came uncertainty about the other. The writer Edwin Muir had noted this as early as the 1930s, when he toured his homeland for the book *Scottish Journey*:

I should like to put here my main impression, and it is that Scotland is gradually being emptied of its population, its spirit, its wealth, industry, art, intellect and innate character.

Muir, being a politicised Scot, naturally had an agenda of his own – he dreamed of a Scotland 'freed from capitalism'. My edition of the book dates from 1985 and includes an introduction by T C Smout, who taught me Economic History in my second year at Edinburgh University. Smout says this of Muir's quest:

So where did Muir's personal quest for the Scottish identity leave him? Not with one clear picture, but with many impressions. There was no distinctive Scotland in Edinburgh, none worth having in small town life, none that could breathe humanity in the oppression of Glasgow, none that rang true in the kailyard [literally 'kitchen-garden'; a sentimental school of Scottish writing] or in the myth-making of Christopher Grieve [the poet Hugh MacDiarmid]. There was instead a deeply disunited people, depressed rather than oppressed, quick to resent any insult to Scotland but lethargically incapable of taking any action to stop its decline. Yet there were still inhabitants of this smashed and emptied country (emptied of spirit, population and innate character) who called themselves Scots and meant by it to distinguish themselves from other people.

Of course, the further some migrants travel from their homeland, the more they strive to embrace its culture. In the USA, Canada and New Zealand there are living-rooms decorated with tartan wallpaper and homes with subscriptions to the *Sunday Post* and the *Scots Magazine*. The first time I ever drank out of a quaich (the traditional Scots sharing-cup), it had been offered to me by an American. The first Highland Games I ever attended was a few years ago in Scottsdale, Arizona. I ate mutton pies and drank Irn-Bru there, and watched people buying claymores and shields. In my own books, I've noticed that Scots words started creeping in around the time I was planning to leave London for south-west France. My father had recently died, and this may have had some bearing on my actual choice of words: 'wersh', 'keech', 'peching' and 'shoogly' were favourites of his. All of them appear in *Strip Jack*, published in 1992 and probably started in 1990, the year of his death. I'd grown up thinking books had to be written in Standard English. The writings of James Kelman had shown me this needn't be the case. Now, as I began flitting to France, I decided to take my Fife vocabulary with me, keeping it alive by using it in my stories. I still don't write continuously in Scots. This is, again, down to my father, who'd found Kelman's linguistic experiments heavy-going. Anxious not to alienate too many readers, I use Scottish words sparingly, measuring them for their effect and ensuring that context explains them to outsiders.

So when a word I've used ends up in the *Shorter Oxford English Dictionary*, alongside a quote from one of my books to explain it, I get a real buzz. In fact, I'm fair chuffed.

Writing recently, Stuart Cosgrove got into trouble for daring to suggest, in one newspaper's phrase, that the Scots 'celebrate failure and poverty', having been blighted by an industrial 'tsunami'. 'We expect decline,' Cosgrove says, 'We expect failure.' And our current literature (the novels of Kelman and Irvine Welsh were cited) wallows in this – or at the very least reflects it. In other words, the collapse of once-treasured industries has left deep psychological scars. But who are these scarred people? Who are the Scots? The commentator Joyce McMillan said this:

> The only definitions of national atmosphere or identity that even begin to work are incremental, pluralistic, paradoxical, open-ended and creative; they aspire to the condition of poetry or theatre, rather than politics or logic.

Joyce was writing in *Holyrood*, the house magazine of the Scottish Parliament. I'd like to think that the Rebus series, taken as a whole, fulfils at least some of her requirements. A single work such as the present one will struggle to define Scotland or Scottishness. The Scottish spirit is thrawn and contrary – as was Christopher Grieve, who strived always to be 'whaur extremes meet' and said he would 'hae nae haufway hoose'. He was expelled from the SNP for being a Communist, and from the Communist Party for being a Nat! This is classic contrariness

We'll hae nae hauf-way hoose.

and can be applied to many Scots. We do not fit easy categories. This is
why I keep finding new things to say about Rebus: he remains full of
surprises. It delighted me to find that Rebus himself has roots outside
Scotland. My own mother was born and raised in Yorkshire, my wife
was born in England but grew up in Northern Ireland (through the
worst of the Troubles). My two sons were born in France, but are growing up in Scotland. In his book about whisky, *Raw Spirit*, Iain Banks
says that the Scots are 'the result of a great blending and marrying over
the millennia'. His use of 'blending' is perfect, and may explain some of
the kinks in our national character. What Scotland needs now more
than anything is a revived confidence concerning its place in the
world. For centuries we defined ourselves in terms of a negative, by
always referring to our neighbours south of the border: 'Who are the
Scots? Well, we're not English.' In the same vein, a regular toast at get-
togethers is: 'Here's tae us, wha's like us? Gey few and they're a' deid!'
Again, this is reductive. We deserve something more, and look to our
revitalised parliament for guidance.

The parliament, however, has had problems of its own. Over-
budget and of radical design, people have been slow to warm to the
actual building. Many think that it sits on the wrong site and doesn't
look right. On the other hand, its position opposite the Palace of
Holyrood could hardly be more apposite: the new going head to
head with the old. What the Royal Family make of it during their
stays in Edinburgh is anyone's guess. I took Rebus to the parliament
in *Set In Darkness* precisely so I could discuss a pivotal moment in
Scottish history. I also took him there because, having learned that
an act of cannibalism had taken place on the same site, it was too
good an opportunity to miss. In decrying success, and striving for
the same 'aggressive egalitarianism' ascribed to Knox and the Ulster
Scots, we are ourselves in danger of committing a kind of cultural
cannibalism, allowing no room for dissent and free expression,
always fearing the worst from any initiative or innovation, clinging
to the wreckage of the past.

Haunted by his past, Rebus is typical of a sort of Scottishness:
brooding and filled with guilt. He sees salvation in neither the secular
nor the religious (though from time to time he seeks it in both). Here he

is at the end of *Resurrection Men*, having completed a gruelling case which has brought him too close to his nemesis, Cafferty:

> *I've made a pact with the devil*, he thought as his hands gripped the edge of the breakfast table. Resurrection would only come to those who deserved it; Rebus knew he was not among them. He could find a church and pray all he liked, or offer up his confession to Strathern. Neither would make a jot of difference. *This* was how the jobs got done: with a tainted conscience, guilty deals, and complicity. With grubby motives and a spirit grown corrupt. His steps were so shallow as he walked towards the door, he could have been wearing shackles.

Those shackles are difficult to break.

Rebus's chains, however, are linked to those worn by Morris Gerald Cafferty himself. Having made a cameo appearance in *Tooth and Nail*, Cafferty's personality demanded a more substantial role. I've called him Rebus's nemesis; some commentators have compared him with Moriarty in the Sherlock Holmes books. There may be something in this: despite their mutual loathing, Holmes and Moriarty share a grudging respect for one another's skills and wiliness. Holmes's psychological make-up certainly takes him closer to Moriarty than to a character like Watson. The subtext seems to be that the skills needed to be a great detective are also those required by a master criminal.

Cafferty himself is not based on any real-life criminal. Edinburgh isn't large enough to merit a gangland-style 'Mr Big'. He's more an amalgam of various Glasgow godfathers of the past. Rather than envisage Edinburgh's underworld run by a dozen small-time operators, I decided that Cafferty could usefully represent a fair proportion of illegal activities. He remains 'old school', however, with his own code of honour, and thus is under threat from younger, less scrupled thugs (as in *The Hanging Garden*). I'm never sure with Rebus and Cafferty whether they're going to become friends, or end up in a fight to the death. They're two sides of the same coin: similar ages and backgrounds; both feeling like dinosaurs as the world around them changes. Rebus may feel that he's made a pact with the devil.

To which I say: better the devil you know.

OVERLEAF: Glasgow reborn.

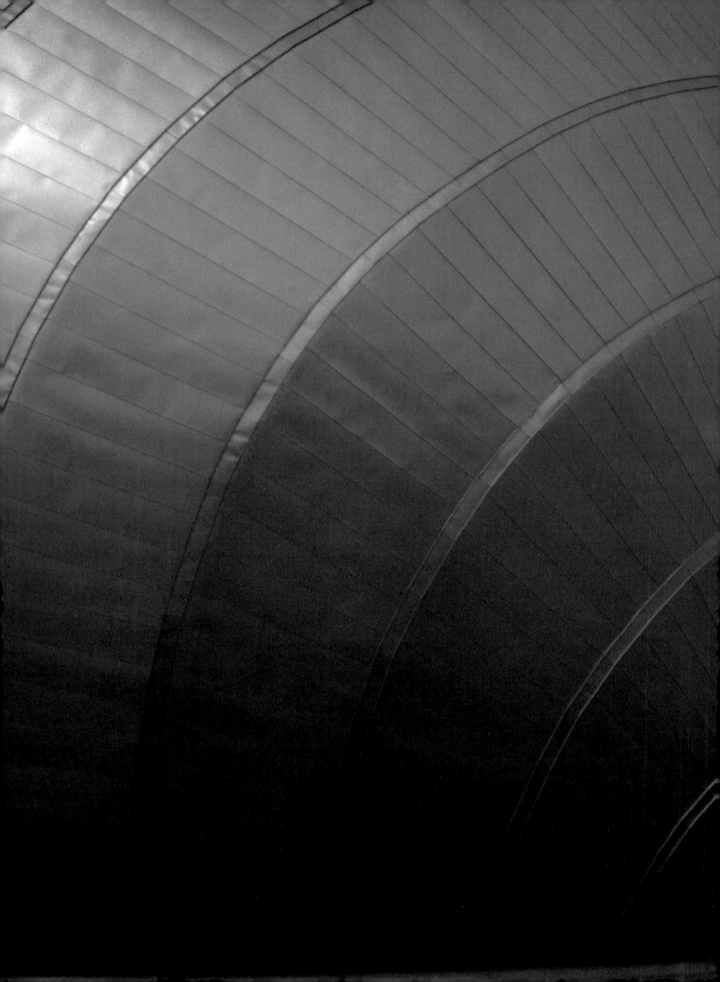

4

Through a Glass Darkly

THE SCOTTISH TV COMEDY SHOW *Chewing the Fat* features a recurring sketch where a reluctant toper is urged to 'take a drink'. The community around him will not be appeased until he indulges, like them, in alcohol. This goes deep into the psyche of the Scot. We bond in drink, throw off our customary reticence, and are suspicious of non-subscribers.

I was probably eleven or twelve when a New Year visitor to our house, maybe not out of his teens himself, tried to persuade me to take an illicit swig from his bottle of whisky. He was confident I would crave that forbidden taste. The thing was, he was years too late. Neither of my parents was a great drinker, but a bottle of whisky was kept in the pantry for visitors (there was probably a bottle of sherry in there, too). When I was eight or nine, I would sneak into the pantry and take the occasional sip – never very much, but eventually the level in the bottle fell to the extent that my father came to my bedroom one night to ask if I was the culprit. I readily admitted the crime. I had 'prior' after all: my parents saved sixpences in an empty Dimple whisky bottle, and I had gone through a phase of stealing these and leaving them dotted around the house. My dad gave me a good talking to on both occasions, and also started marking the label of the whisky bottle.

During the 1960s, he had brought home treasures from the grocer's shop. On the window-ledge in my bedroom stood a handsome collection of promotional items, including a porcelain white horse (advertising White Horse whisky) and a foot-high, detailed statue of Mr Johnnie Walker himself, complete with top hat, walking-cane and monocle. Is it any wonder I wanted to taste this stuff that dreams were made of? (My dad also brought boxes of chocolate biscuits home, but that's another story.)

Friday nights were when my dad went out with his cronies. For a while, I insisted that he visit my bedroom on his return, so I could

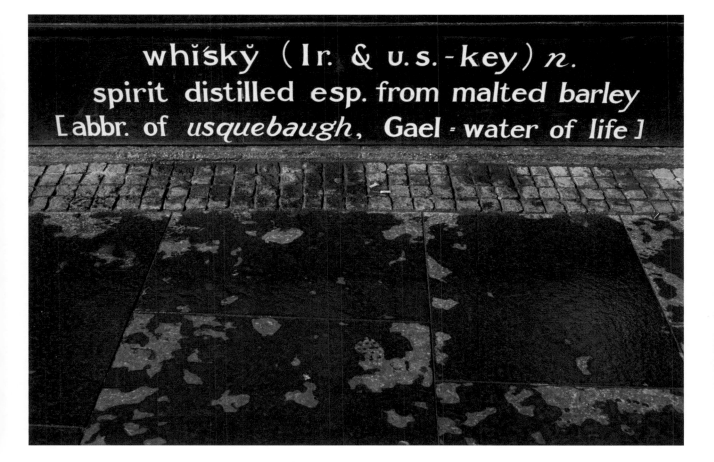

whisky (Ir. & u.s. -key) *n.*
spirit distilled esp. from malted *barley*
[abbr. of *usquebaugh*, Gael - water of *life*]

check he wasn't drunk. Why I did this I've no idea. I probably saw my father drunk on only half a dozen occasions, face merry, lacking any bluster or belligerence. These were usually family affairs: New Year gatherings and weddings. My own rite of passage came when I was seventeen. That Hogmanay, I had my own New Year's bottle (Southern Comfort). Bars had started serving me the previous year; I don't recall ever being turned away or asked for proof of age. On a school trip to Switzerland, some of us had managed to buy duty free booze on board the ferry. Our teacher discovered this and made us promise to hide it away in our hotel room and take it home with us unopened. She relented, however, on the final night of our stay, and came to our room for a snifter, leaving soon after in less sanguine mood when we admitted we'd already necked the lot . . .

Oxford Bar interior.

I had one aunt who lived near us and drank only cherry brandy, insisting it was not alcoholic. Another aunt always seemed very quiet and mousy to me, but came out of her shell at one wedding reception when, after a few too many Sweetheart stouts, she helped me treat the company to a skittish rendition of 'There's a Hole in My Bucket'. Near the start of *The Falls*, Rebus is at Farmer Watson's retirement party when a fellow detective, Bobby Hogan, suggests that the pair of them regale the company with this same song. This is shortly before Rebus, in his cups by now, gets into trouble by turning up at the home of a missing teenager . . .

Rebus has had a problem with drink from the word go. I was probably thinking of all those American private eye films, the bottle of bourbon brought out to freshen a client's glass. And Rebus had a good reason to drink: there were things in his past he needed to forget. In *Knots and Crosses*, booze sees him stagger into bed with a female inebriate, whom he nearly attacks. Later on, in *Dead Souls*, Farmer Watson prepares for a funeral by pouring two stiff drinks:

Rebus nodded, watching the man pour. Cascading sound of mountain streams. *Usquebaugh* in the Gaelic. *Uisge*: water; *beatha*: life. Water of life. *Beatha* sounding like 'birth'. Each drink was a birth to Rebus's mind. But as his doctor kept telling him, each drop was a little death, too.

Some of my favourite descriptions in the books involve bars and the people who drink in them:

> Old men sat with their half-pint glasses, staring emptily towards the front door. Were they wondering what was outside? Or were they just scared that whatever was out there would one day force its way in?

> He'd quietened down, gone all sulky in a corner, standing there with head bent under the weight of a cigarette. The pint glass seemed heavy, too, so that his wrist sagged beneath it, beer dripping down on to his shoes and the wooden floor.

The first of these quotations comes from *Knots and Crosses*, written between the ages of twenty-four and twenty-five. It shows that its young author was well-acquainted with traditional drinking dens, and with the reasons why his jaded elders might frequent them. A pub, at its best, is a place of safety, a retreat from the world. It offers sanctuary, comedy, space for reflection, and the makings of a hangover. It's a place to meet people, or to be alone; a place of vivid conversation or silent reflection. Some of my favourites have been swept away – knocked down in some cases, or changing hands and being transformed into 'style bars'. The character of a bar has much to do with its clientele, but that clientele can be fickle, and changes to the fabric of the bar can cause them to head elsewhere.

In the sleeve notes to some of his albums, singer-songwriter Jackie Leven usually acknowledges a debt to bars which have sustained him through touring and writing. Most of these are real, though I'm doubtful of the veracity of the 'Fuckin Bastard' in Dundee, to give one example. In similar vein, I began the Rebus series writing about semi-fictitious bars with names such as the Sutherland. However, I'd also started drinking at the Oxford Bar, a small and wilfully 'clubby' place not far from Princes Street, yet so wonderfully hidden away that strangers seldom stumbled upon it. One of the students I was sharing a flat with was a regular there (and part-time barman). By my second or third visit, the other bar staff could pour my choice of beer unprompted. I was busy meantime making friends, and discovering that among the clientele were a number of serving and retired police officers.

Perfect.

The Oxford Bar was first identified by name in *Mortal Causes*. Rebus liked its atmosphere and the fact that it sold 'quarter gills' (ie: larger measures of spirits than in most pubs). Even when he stops drinking for a time, however, as happens in *The Hanging Garden*, he continues to haunt the place:

A pub like the Ox was about so much more than just the hooch.
It was therapy and refuge, entertainment and art.

By this stage in the life of the series, I'd decided to use real locations as much as possible, and this extended to the characters themselves. Harry, mentioned in the books as 'Edinburgh's rudest barman . . . quite a feat, considering the competition', really was the barman at the Ox (he now owns the place, and is only rude to a choice few of us who've known him for some time). In *Resurrection Men* I even make reference to Willie Ross, who was the real-life owner of the place a few decades back, and in *Set In Darkness* I make use of a number of real drinkers, too, including Muir, Hayden and Gordon (first names only, to protect the guilty), plus other real bars I've been known to frequent, such as the Maltings and Swany's.

This helps give the books a sense of verisimilitude, plus it's easier for me than having to make places up.

By the time I reached high school, there was a culture of drinking at break-times. Boys would take it in turns to bring a 'mixture' in their satchel. This comprised any kind of container – including on at least one occasion an unwashed ketchup bottle – filled with a mix of decanted spirits from the parental drinks cabinet. A good 'mixture' might be unequal parts dark rum, gin, vodka, whisky and crème de menthe. The container would be passed around until empty. One of my friends keeled over in the chemistry lab after a lunchtime session, but this was put down to heat-stroke, fortunately for the rest of us.

School discos and Christmas dances would be preceded by a few tipples in the cemetery – usually Woodpecker cider, cans of Special Brew, and vodka diluted with some sweetened orange juice (this last a forerunner of today's alcopops). The occasions made us garrulous and brotherly.

And angry.

And ill.

John Gates, who ran the
Oxford Bar until recently.
My pathologist in the
books, Professor Gates,
is named after him.

Non-alcoholic drinks
can also be found
in some places.

One night, after a session at a friend's house, I stumbled home drunk, tried to make my way upstairs to the toilet, but was found by my mother just as my gorge started to rise. Another scolding.

My background is Rebus's, therefore he probably shared at least a few of my underage adventures. But he left school at fifteen and joined the Army – with its macho culture fuelled, in part, by prodigious intake of alcohol. Maybe his serious drinking started there; or maybe it's his Scottishness that makes him 'take a drink', even when he doesn't really feel like one. During his short period of abstinence (between *Black and Blue* and *The Hanging Garden*) he carried with him a bottle of the hard stuff – a little 'grenade' of sorts. And it was this grenade he turned to when forced to face the fact of his daughter's hit-and-run.

So is drink a lazy substitute for Rebus? A way of dealing with problems and stresses? If so, then he's to all intents an alcoholic, but I think his relationship to alcohol is slightly more complex:

One of the reasons Rebus drank was to put him to sleep.

He had trouble sleeping when sober. He'd stare into the darkness, willing it to form shapes so that he might better understand it. He'd try to make sense of life – his early disastrous Army years; his failed marriage; his failings as father, friend, lover – and end up in tears. And if he did eventually stumble into sober sleep, there would be troubled dreams, dreams about ageing and dying, decay and blight . . . Drunk, his sleep was dreamless, or seemed that way on waking   (*Let It Bleed*).

The word for this is 'maudlin', but it reflects a potential problem in many of us. There are millions of people out there who drink to excess at the end of the working week in order to blot out the memories of that same week. Stressed professionals lock the door behind them and reach for the corkscrew or the gin. Rebus is no different, except that he is not a social drinker. Even when in company, he's not really of the company. He's always alone with his thoughts and his personal demons, and he drinks despite his work, not because of it:

Police routine gave his daily life its only shape and substance; it gave him a schedule to work to, a reason to get up in the morning. He loathed his free time, dreaded Sundays off. He lived to work, and in a very real sense he worked to live, too: the much-maligned Protestant work ethic. Subtract work from the equation and the day became flabby, like releasing jelly from its mould. Besides, without work, what reason had he not to drink?   (*Let It Bleed*).

In *Scottish Journey*, Edwin Muir sums up the national attitude to alcohol in this way:

Scottish people drink spasmodically and intensely, for the sake of a momentary but complete release, whereas the English like to bathe and paddle about bucolically in a mild puddle of beer.

Several things strike me about this. One is that Muir is describing the Scots very much as binge-drinkers. Another is that he could just as easily be describing an addiction to hard drugs ('a momentary but complete release'), as portrayed in novels such as the Edinburgh-based *Trainspotting*. Thirdly, were he alive today and visiting any town of size in England on a Friday night, he might wish to revise his opinion of that 'mild puddle'. In retreading Muir's steps half a century later, James Campbell mentions 'the monotonous peacefulness common to all Scottish small towns, which in the evening turns to eerie silence, punctuated by the sounds of children and drunks'.

Nowadays, however, the drunks themselves are likely to be children, their punctuations replacing any trace of silence. Yet while our cities' night-time streets are alive with drunks, I see little obvious drunkenness in places like the Oxford Bar. It seems to have its own unwritten rules, and somehow these are obeyed. The government-sanctioned phrase 'Drink Responsibly' might have been thought up after a quiet session in the back room of the Ox. I've only once encountered violence over its threshold (and that ruck involved journalists, for whom no rules are sacred). The same can be said for the other bars I've been known to visit throughout Scotland. My favourite in Glasgow is the Horseshoe:

It was central and crowded with people who took their drinking seriously, the kind of place where no one looked askance at a tea-stained shirt, so long as the wearer had about him the price of his drink. Rebus knew immediately that it would be a place of rules and rituals, a place where regulars would know from the moment they walked through the door that their drink of preference was already being poured for them   (*Resurrection Men*)

I could just as well be describing the Oxford Bar.

My only rule in choosing these watering-holes has been: never drink in a bar with bouncers on the door. If they're expecting trouble, trouble is probably on its way.

Aggression and alcohol go fist in hand, of course, and there's something in the Scottish psyche that makes us prone to dark thoughts when drunk, and occasionally dark deeds, too. One of the theories of *Dr Jekyll and Mr Hyde* (that most Edinburgh of novels, yet infuriatingly set in London) is that it refers to its author's drunken exploits in the stews of his native city. Robert Louis Stevenson was born into a respectable professional family, and lived in what remains one of the finest streets in Edinburgh, yet as a young man he was hungry to explore another side of his character, a side unleashed during visits to the rough-houses in the chaotic maze of the Old Town (he himself lived in the rational and well-ordered 'New Town'). One of the frontispieces to this current book shows Stevenson's exaggerated version of the Edinburgh he knew. He's describing the worsening condition of the Old Town, the encroaching 'sordidness' and lawlessness bringing policemen to the scene.

To this day alcohol remains one of the main generators of 'domestic crime', a world away from the distillery tours enjoyed by Iain Banks in his travel book *Raw Spirit*. (Banks' choice of title, as usual, has a double meaning: he discusses the raw spirit of the Scots along the way.)

The rich relationship between the Scots and alcohol goes beyond our invention of whisky, and drips down into the language. We possess myriad words for drunkenness: hoolit, steaming, guttered, wellied, blootered. The word 'mingin' was current in Scotland well before it entered the lexicon south of the border. We call alcohol 'bevvy', short for 'beverage', turning it into a euphemism. We go to the pub for a 'wee swallie' (a small swallow). The pub culture of the British Isles is pretty well unique. Pubs are our social clubs. A good 'local' may include its own darts team or quiz team. Golf tournaments may be organised,

The cells at St Leonard's.

This lap-dancing bar is named after the
notorious Edinburgh murderers and is
sited not far from The Nook, my fictitious
establishment in *Fleshmarket Close*.

along with trips abroad for rugby matches. The landlord stands each and every regular a free drink at New Year, and when those same regulars head off on holiday, they send postcards which are displayed behind the bar. In this way, the pub becomes a surrogate home, its drinkers a kind of family – dysfunctional, to be sure, but tight-knit.

This is another reason why Rebus drinks. He has no family around him, and precious few friends. Bars suit that side of the Scottish character which is reticent and introverted. They're places where you can be as invisible as you like. At the same time, they are also confessionals. I've had near-strangers tell me their innermost secrets after one too many drinks. They say it can be easier to talk to strangers than to one's own close family, and this seems to be the case. Of course, not all bars offer similar comforts. In Glasgow, there are Rangers pubs and Celtic pubs, and the unwitting visitor must be careful not to make the wrong choice. Drinkers in most places are territorial anyway, wary of the new face. You could be an undercover cop or a social security spy. I once walked into a bar in Uig on the Isle of Skye, and the change in atmosphere was immediate and unsettling. If someone had been playing the piano, they would have ceased. In my memory, the barman was drying pint-glasses with a towel, like a scene from a cowboy film. When I asked for Talisker, the local malt, the murmur of conversation started up again. I'd selected the correct password.

It probably was little different in Stevenson's day. Many of the scenes I describe in my books seem to me timeless. Here's Rebus, encountering Cafferty late one night in the Royal Oak, a bar renowned for its live music. Cafferty is regaling the place with a rendition of a Burns song:

Deacon Brodie's is named after the infamous Edinburgh character who influenced *Jekyll and Hyde*.

One of the barmaids took Rebus's order: a half of Eighty and a whisky. There was no conversation in the bar, respectful silence and even a tear in one patriot's eye as she sat on her stool with her brandy and Coke raised to her lips, her ragged boyfriend stroking her shoulders from behind.

When the song finished, there was applause, a few whistles and cheers. Cafferty bowed his head, lifted his whisky glass and toasted the room. As the clapping subsided, the accordionist took it as his cue to commence . . . (*Set In Darkness*)

This is a Scotland Stevenson would surely recognise – maudlin to a degree (that tearful 'patriot'), democratic in its respect of anyone's right to sing a song, and with an acknowledgement of the ephemeral nature of existence (the way Cafferty's singing melts into the next musical act). In centuries past, Scotland's 'howffs' and oyster bars were places where the rich and poor could mingle – something not possible in the hierarchical world outside. Poets, ruffians and harlots could be found there. The poet Robert Fergusson wrote with almost filmic quality of Edinburgh's low life in the eighteenth century, a time when thirty million oysters a year would be taken from the Forth estuary to accompany the citizens' various tipples. These bars were ideal locations for cops. If the culprit couldn't be found there, someone with some inside gen might be persuaded to talk over a free drink. Writers share some similarities with detectives: we have questions about the world that need answering; we look to our fellow humans, seeking motives and wondering about their secret lives. And like detectives, writers have always enjoyed the drinking life, bars our private studies. We find characters there, and stories, and themes. We covet anecdotes and linguistic gems. The best pubs show us Scotland in miniature, with all its uncertainties, problems and joie de vivre.

As I write, there are moves by the Scottish Executive towards an outright ban on smoking in bars, clubs and restaurants. If alcohol has taken its toll on the Scots, then so have cigarettes. When a similar ban was imposed in Ireland, it was said it would never work. Scotland's First Minister, however, was energised after a visit to Dublin. In many pubs in Scotland, a pint and a 'fag' go hand in hand (as it were). In the early novels, Rebus is trying to rein in his nicotine consumption, aware that he is killing himself by degrees. By the later novels, however, his cravings have the better of him. I grew up with two parents who smoked into their fifties. Both eventually gave up, and maybe Rebus can be persuaded to do the same. Otherwise, he will have to step out of the warm, well-lit Oxford Bar and into the inhospitable Edinburgh night for his regular fix.

I prefaced my novel *Let It Bleed* with a quotation from Martin Amis's *Money*: 'Without women, life is a pub.' Hard to tell if Amis's narrator thinks this a good thing; John Rebus certainly finds his local howff a suitable alternative.

Just one more small part of his failing.

The Guildford Arms, upon which I based my fictional pub The Sutherland in the early novels.

5

Does Rebus Like the Cure?

PUNK CAME ALONG at just the right time for me. I was seventeen in 1977. That December, at the Christmas dance at my high school, a number of us went onstage to provide some live music. I forget what we called ourselves, but the song we'd rehearsed was a bastardised version of 'London's Burning' by The Clash. It was called 'Cowdenbeath's Burning' and the lyrics had something to do with a strike protest being undertaken by the town's firemen. I sang my own lyrics, while our guitarist (trained in jazz and classical) provided an overly elegant and lengthy solo. After our semi-raucous performance, I decided not to change out of my punk fancy-dress. A novelty dance was announced, with ladies choosing their partners. My friend Anne chose me, despite the fact that one of her legs was encased in a cast – the result of an accident. As the dance progressed, the gentlemen were told to pick up their partners and carry them across an invisible river with all due speed. Halfway across, I felt myself start to fall, my arms trapped beneath my partner. My chin hit the floor and split open. I ended the dance with a trip to A&E and three stitches in my jaw. I was still dressed as a punk when the headmaster drove me home. (Don't worry; Anne was fine.)

Earlier in the year, I'd tried putting together a local version of the fanzine *Sniffing Glue*, sneaking into the Economics department to photocopy my badly typed sheets. Eventually, a proper school magazine emerged, using my suggested title of *Mainlines*. In our first issue, a friend wrote a detailed review of the local bars, while I contributed a piece on . . . well, probably The Clash again. Our moment of glory, however, came when a letter and photo we sent to the London-based music weekly *Sounds* ended up in print. The photo showed our prototype band in casual pose at the urinals in the school toilets. The sub-editor gave us the heading 'Scottish Loonies Department'. We were absolutely thrilled.

Meantime, Stuart Adamson, who had been a couple of years above me at Beath, was enjoying success with his band The Skids. (Later, he would enjoy a further, brief triumph with Big Country, before eventually committing suicide.) Some of us would head down to Kirkcaldy on a Sunday night to the Pogo-A-Gogo Club, which The Skids often played. I worked school holidays in a chicken hatchery, and had purloined one of the blue boiler-suits, laying it out on my bedroom carpet and pouring neat bleach over it. Two problems with this: one, it reeked whenever I worked up a sweat; two, it left a large white stain on the carpet . . . I would sneak my punk gear out of the house and remodel myself in a friend's bathroom, after which his bemused father would drive us the five miles to our destination . . . and pick us up again afterwards. It was too dangerous for punks to wait for buses: one of our number had been head-butted by a guy wearing a crash-helmet . . .

In my first year at Edinburgh University, I joined a new wave band called The Dancing Pigs, formed by another ex-school friend. We sounded like an uneasy mix of Japan, Joy Division and The Skids, and only lasted six months. Time enough to work the rock'n'roll bug out of my system, but also leaving a lasting impression that anything was possible if you had confidence. As punk had proved, you didn't need much in the way of technical ability; it could be replaced with any amount of *chutzpah*.

The Scots phrase for it is 'being gallus'.

I was gallus enough to send my fledgling poetry to anyone and everyone: the *Listener* and *Literary Review*, *TLS* and *Scotsman*. Not even the *Economist* was safe. And though none of these publications ever touched my work with anything shorter than a bargepole, the confidence instilled by punk never left me.

I'd been into music long before punk, of course. The first proper single I ever bought was probably 'Double Barrel' by Dave and Ansil Collins, purchased just shy of my eleventh birthday. (I'm not counting the 'Action Man' theme song, which preceded this by a year or two.) In my last year at primary school, I discovered *Sounds*, with its free centre-spread colour poster. Many bands graced my bedroom walls

The jacket for my book
Beggars Banquet, its title
borrowed from the
Rolling Stones.

The old meat market in
Edinburgh's Stockbridge,
near where Nico was rumoured
to be living while I was
in student digs along the road.

before their products ever graced my Dansette turntable (actually my sister's, bought for her with cigarette-coupons collected by our mum and dad). As recounted at the start of *The Black Book*, Rebus used to own a Dansette, too. My sister and I would have to add coins to the pick-up to stop the stylus from jumping. Linda didn't have much of a record collection: Simon and Garfunkel, The Beatles and the Corries; the soundtracks to *Mary Poppins* and *The Sound of Music*. There was a Dubliners song we'd sing together about a drunkard being cuckolded by his wife. There would be Radio One as we readied for school (Tony Blackburn DJing, aided by a fictitious dog called Arnold), and the Black and White Minstrels on the television at night, plus occasional party-pieces at Uncle Math's two doors away, folk standards played on his 'moothie' (harmonica). I was twelve when Linda got married. The reception was at the local Masonic Hall. I'd conscientiously prepared my 'turn' – a rendition of 'The Boxer' from *Bridge Over Troubled Water*, even though the resident accordionist tried to dissuade me on the night . . .

T Rex and Alice Cooper sustained me for a time. Then came Bowie, Roxy Music and Frank Zappa. By high school, I was swapping albums daily with like-minded individuals, stretching my horizons to include ELP, Yes and Gong. On one fateful night, I decided to go and see post-Peter Gabriel Genesis in Edinburgh, rather than Rory Gallagher.

We learn through our mistakes.

I started to bring music into the books because I'm still a frustrated rock star at heart, but also because, to my mind, a person's musical taste says a lot about them. If you're new to the Rebus books, you can ascertain his age, class and personality from his listening choices. Leonard Cohen, for example, is not much listened to by gregarious, outgoing types, while a liking for mid-period Stones indicates that Rebus is working class, thinks himself a bit of a rebel, and is probably in his fifties. There is, however, a hidden agenda in the roster of artists I choose to write about, and this is where Siobhan comes in. The thing is, being younger than Rebus, I don't always share his tastes. You need to add Rebus and Siobhan together to get a more accurate picture of my own favourites, and many of these are Scottish. Deacon Blue, Edwyn Collins, Mogwai, Oldsolar, The Blue Nile, The Bathers and

Glasgow's Barrowland Ballroom, latterly a rock venue but also the haunt of *Black and Blue*'s Bible John.

Jackie Leven all feature in the books. Even my own band, The Dancing Pigs, are given a cameo in *Black and Blue*. I've also managed to flag up that three of the most influential bands of all time – The Beatles, Stones and Cream – featured Scottish members at some crucial point.

By strange coincidence, I needed a band for *Set In Darkness* and decided to call them Obscura – named for Edinburgh's Camera Obscura where, legend has it, Donald Cammell (director of such underground classics as *Performance*) was born. Around the same time, a Scottish band called Camera Obscura came into being, in one of those cases of serendipity which have attended most of my literary output. My band Obscura needed album titles, and I gifted them *Continuous Repercussions* – the title of an album by a band I'd invented as a twelve-year old. (The band were called The Amoebas, and existed only in my notebooks. Their lead singer was called Ian Kaput – not that I was living a fantasy or anything . . .)

It's not just rock either. Two great jazz artists, Carol Kidd and Tommy Smith, make appearances in the books (though Carol only through a song title). This was easier early on in the series, when Rebus listened to jazz and even – at one point – classical music! I had extensive knowledge of neither genre: I just figured this was the sort of stuff existential loner cops would play. In similar vein, Rebus is too articulate and literate in those first few novels. He thinks as I would, rather than as a middle-aged detective would. He can quote Walt Whitman and Shakespeare, reads Dostoevsky, and dips into the Book of Job. On the other hand, the future course of his musical taste was hinted at by the very first musical reference in *Knots and Crosses* – 'Wipe Out' by Surfaris. Though I probably didn't realise it at the time, this song would almost certainly have been on Rebus's shopping-list on its release in the summer of 1963 (I didn't hear it until ten years later).

In later books, there are oblique references to Frank Zappa (a favourite of mine during university), Jethro Tull, David Bowie and Van Morrison. Rebus even attends several gigs at which I, too, was present, including Barclay James Harvest at the Usher Hall (my first concert, actually), Tom Waits at the Playhouse, and even The Fall at a club in the Abbeyhill area of Edinburgh. I've no idea what he would have made of The Fall . . .

Abbeymount in Edinburgh, close to the venue where I saw The Fall.

Music is mentioned to such an extent in the books that *Private Eye*, reviewing one instalment, said my stories were just excuses to trawl my record collection and offset the whole thing against tax. I hope there's a little more to it than that:

> He went over to the hi-fi. After a drink, he liked to listen to the Stones. Women, relationships and colleagues had come and gone, but the Stones had always been there. He put the album on and poured himself a last drink. The guitar riff, one of easily half a dozen in Keith's tireless repertoire, kicked the album off. I don't have much, Rebus thought, but I have this   (*Let It Bleed*, p 38).

Rebus also owns the same Nakamichi tape-deck I used to cherish (it was stolen during a break-in at my Tottenham flat), and several times in the course of the series I sneak in mentions of Linn hi-fi components. A character in *Hide and Seek* owns some, and Rebus tries to buy a Linn system in *The Falls*. As happened to me in real life, Rebus is knocked back by the assistant, who probably reckons the shabbily dressed, beery customer cannot afford the goods.

I spent a couple of years working in London for a hi-fi magazine, reviewing top-end equipment. The job was fun. (Fellow author Lee Child often jokes that he was my first reader, having been a fan of the magazine.) The staff of *Hi-Fi Review* saw Linn as the holy grail of audio reproduction, which made me distinctly proud, Linn being based in Glasgow. I eventually saved up the money for one of their turntables, was privileged to visit their HQ, and met their founder, Ivor Tiefenbrun, several times. On a trip to London, it was Ivor who told me I should move back to Scotland.

'I might end up in Edinburgh,' I agreed.

'That's not Scotland,' he said, pulling a face, and reinforcing the jokey antipathy common between Scotland's two main cities.

One of my jobs as a hi-fi reviewer entailed taking the equipment to pieces to see just how well-made it was. I recall unscrewing the bass cone from a Linn loudspeaker and peering inside, finding myself confronted by a single word stamped within the cabinet, where no purchaser would ever see it. The word was 'Clydebuilt', harking back to

Glasgow's industrial past. Here were people so proud of their abilities that they had to leave a mark on each product, a secret sign of their success.

Again, this seems typically Scottish: the pride has to remain hidden, lest it look like boasting. Maybe this explains Scotland's relative failure in terms of popular music. We can claim the likes of Lulu and the Bay City Rollers, Simple Minds and Rod Stewart, but most of our bands specialise in left-field sounds, making them cult listening rather than stadium pleasers. In *A Question of Blood* Rebus lists his 'top three Scottish acts': Nazareth, Alex Harvey, Deacon Blue. Then goes on to add John Martyn, Jack Bruce, Ian Anderson, Donovan, the Incredible String Band, Maggie Bell, Frankie Miller and Jackie Leven. As lists go, it's not bad, and Siobhan might add the likes of Mogwai, Josef K, the Cocteau Twins and Belle and Sebastian (this last actually voted Best Scottish Band Ever in a recent magazine poll). The Scottish music scene is too eclectic, too disparate actually to be called a 'scene'.

My feeling is that Rebus likes the Stones ('Stonehenge with a blues riff', as he calls them in *Black and Blue* – itself the title of one of their albums) not only because they have provided a constancy in his life, but because they are survivors. As someone once said, the only living creatures to survive all-out nuclear war would be some scorpions . . . and Keith Richards. Rebus, too, is a survivor of whatever life throws at him. He respects musicians who have 'earned their chops', people like Van Morrison and John Martyn. He's also, it has to be said, wary of change. He cannot get his head around new technology (which, in the books, gives Siobhan a chance to show that she's every bit as good a detective as him, but with a different set of skills). I'm betting he's a fan of Status Quo, too – the band as well as the attitude. In *A Question of Blood* he finds it hard to comprehend the new Goth culture, represented by 'Miss Teri', a teenager who dresses in black and hangs around Cockburn Street with like-minded Goths. Two of my three favourite record shops, Fopp and Avalanche, sit on Cockburn Street (the other, Backbeat on East Crosscauseway, may be the maddest emporium in the UK, filled to the brim and beyond with obscure vinyl and oldies). Whenever I visit those two shops, I have to weave my way through pockets of baggy-trousered, whey-faced teens, maybe feeling the way Rebus felt when,

South Queensferry, setting for *A Question of Blood*.

back in the late-1970s, he encountered his first punks on that same thoroughfare:

> Rebus still remembered one Saturday when he'd been out buying records. Starting the long climb up Cockburn Street and passing his first punks: all slouches and spiky hair, chains and sneers. It had been too much for the middle-aged woman behind him, who'd spluttered out the words 'Can't you walk like human beings?', probably making the punks' day in the process   (*A Question of Blood*, p 201).

I can confirm this to have been the case, because I was one of that group, though the woman was actually talking to my mate 'Dauve' (real name Dave), who would later play keyboards in The Dancing Pigs.

A Question of Blood was written prior to the murder of Dalkeith teenager Jodi Jones, and the subsequent conviction of her 'Goth' boyfriend. The case brought out the usual media frenzy. Marilyn Manson's lyrics, artwork and videos were reproduced in court by the prosecution as part of its case, while cannabis was also said to be partly to blame for the killing. Famously, Manson had also been blamed for the Columbine shootings in the USA, his lyric 'I kill who I don't like' being quoted by prosecutors. But people commit murders for all sorts of reasons – in Scotland as elsewhere. Simple, closed solutions satisfy a basic need in human beings for comprehension, but the truth is usually more complex and unattainable, which may explain why I decided that *A Question of Blood* should not end with the solving of each and every one of its mysteries.

My books have brought me closer to musicians. I've had e-mails from REM, Hawkwind and Pete Townshend. Fans of Wishbone Ash discuss my mentions of their heroes on the band's message board. Robin Guthrie (ex-Cocteau Twins, now record label guru) sends me CDs he thinks I might like. Stuart David, bass player with Belle and Sebastian, paid at a charity auction for his alter ego to appear in *A Question of Blood*. (The alter ego is Peacock Johnson, who also stars in Stuart's first novel.) Best of all, however, singer-songwriter Jackie Leven saw his work cited in *Resurrection Men* and made contact with me. Jackie writes eloquently about 'the romantic hard men of Fife' (*A Question of*

OVERLEAF:

Grangemouth, home of the Cocteau Twins.

Blood), their disappointments and small victories. We met and began to work together, eventually producing a show which was recorded for release as an album. A quarter of a century after The Dancing Pigs, the CD of *Jackie Leven Said* was being reviewed in the *Independent* newspaper and *Q* magazine.

A Question of Blood opens with a suicide, and Scottish musicians have not been noted for their longevity. In particular, the deaths (at their own hand) of both Stuart Adamson and Billy Mackenzie saddened me. Both had provided music to my bedsit days and nights, and Adamson's skirling Big Country had been that rarest of Scottish musical beasts – full of confidence and bombast, telling us that we really did live in a big country, a place to be proud of. Ironically the words 'stay alive' provide the refrain to one of his most popular songs. But Scotland was either too much or not enough for him, as for so many of its children before and since.

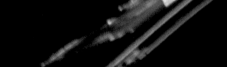

CHIPS - PIZZA & KEB

6

Edinburgh

Princes Street
from Calton Hill.

LIVING IN CARDENDEN as a teenager, I'd written about the place to try to make sense of it. I was asking: how do I fit into the scheme of things? I was also making my hometown seem more exciting and romantic than it really was. And I was playing God, controlling the world of my fictional creations in a way that was impossible in reality.

Moving to Edinburgh in October 1978, it was natural that I would start writing about this strange, complicated city – though to term Edinburgh a 'city' can sometimes seem an exaggeration. With a population of around half a million, it is overshadowed by many conurbations south of the border, and even by its close neighbour Glasgow. Robert Louis Stevenson described his birthplace as 'not so much a small city as the largest of small towns'. I describe it in my books as 'a city the size of a town that thinks like a village'. It's true that Edinburgh can seem claustrophobic at times. Walking through the Cowgate can feel like being at the bottom of a narrow canyon. Live in the place long enough, and it's hard to venture out without bumping into friends and acquaintances. Yet at the same time the city can appear cold and unwelcoming. Visitors note that strangers don't chat at bus stops the way they do in Glasgow or Belfast. Privacy is guarded at all times:

> There were those who said that Edinburgh was an invisible city, hiding its true feelings and intentions, its citizens outwardly respectable, its streets appearing frozen in time. You could visit the place and come away with little sense of having understood what drove it. This was the city of Deacon Brodie, where bridled passions were given free play only at night. The city of John Knox, his rectitude stern and indomitable. You might need half a million pounds to buy one of the better houses, yet outward show was

frowned upon: a city of Saabs and Volvos rather than Bentleys and Ferraris. Glaswegians – who considered themselves more passionate, more Celtic – thought Edinburgh staid and conventional to the point of prissiness.

Hidden city. The historical proof: when invading armies advanced, the populace made themselves scarce in the caves and tunnels below the Old Town. Their homes might be ransacked, but the soldiers would leave eventually – it was hard to enjoy victory without the evidence of the vanquished – and the locals would come back into the light to begin the work of rebuilding.

Out of the darkness and into the light.

The Presbyterian ethos swept idolatry from the churches, but left them strangely empty and echoing, filling them with congregations who'd been told that from birth they were doomed. All of this filtering down through the consciousness of the years. The citizens of Edinburgh made good bankers and lawyers perhaps precisely because they held their emotions in check, and were good at keeping secrets (*Set In Darkness*).

Not that this is always a good thing in Rebus's eyes:

Still nobody had come to investigate, to see what all the noise and the fuss were. Like Edinburghers of old, they could become invisible to trouble. In olden times, they'd hidden in the catacombs below the Castle and the High Street. Now they just shut their windows and turned up the TV. They were Rebus's employers, whose taxes paid his salary. They were the people he was paid to protect. He felt like telling them to all go to hell   (*Mortal Causes*).

In my early books especially I was keen to point out parallels between my work and predecessors such as *Jekyll and Hyde* and *Confessions of a Justified Sinner*. I was an English Literature postgraduate after all, teaching classes of *Ulysses* in my spare time and dreaming of a future professorship – I wanted to be taken seriously as a writer. Living as I had done in a succession of dreary flats, motels and high-rise blocks, yet researching towards my PhD each day in the grand sur-

roundings of the National Library and Central Library, Edinburgh really did seem a divided city. In *Knots and Crosses*, the appearance in the city of a serial killer has reporters dusting off stories about Deacon Brodie (gentleman by day, scoundrel by night), Burke and Hare (who murdered their victims then sold them on to surgeons in the guise of the recently grave-robbed), and hauntings (Edinburgh is said to be one of the most haunted cities in Europe). For Rebus, in that first adventure, Lothian Road is typical of the divided city:

> He was watching from his window as the city's late-night drunks rolled their way up and down the obstacle-strewn hazard of Lothian Road, seeking alcohol, women, happiness. It was a never-ending search for some of them, staggering in and out of clubs and pubs and take-aways, gnawing on the packaged bones of existence. Lothian Road was Edinburgh's dustbin. It was also home to the Sheraton Hotel and the Usher Hall. Rebus had visited the Usher Hall once, sitting with Rhona and the other smug souls listening to Mozart's Requiem Mass. It was typical of Edinburgh to have a crumb of culture sited amidst the fast-food shops. A requiem mass and a bag of chips.

This reflects one of the perennial problems I've had with Mr John Rebus. He is a professional misanthrope, made cynical by the job he does. Every day of his life he moves through an extraordinary city, but dealing only with its victims and miscreants. By the time of the second Rebus novel, *Hide and Seek*, he acknowledges as much:

> He was living in the most beautiful, most civilised city in northern Europe, yet every day had to deal with its flipside.

Many books later, in *The Falls*, when the museum curator Jean Burchill stops to gaze out across the city, Rebus disingenuously nods his agreement at her assessment of its beauty. To him, 'it wasn't a view at all. It was a crime scene waiting to happen.'

Between times, Rebus has had to visit most areas of Edinburgh. In the early books, many of these were fictional. You won't, for example, find a 'Great London Road' (site of Rebus's first police station), though you can go to London Road and guess that I probably meant the station to sit somewhere around there. But right from the start, Rebus lived in a real street – Arden Street. This was the street I was living in when I got the idea for the first book. It's in Marchmont, an area infamous for its students, who seem to irk some of their neighbours by playing music and not taking proper care of the tenements' communal stair-wells. Edinburgh, despite its elegant housing stock and the Georgian splendour of the New Town, remains a city of tenements. People who have never visited the place sometimes think these must be dilapidated affairs (mistaking them, perhaps, for the slum tenements of Glasgow, knocked down in the 1960s). But many of Edinburgh's tenements are clean, well-lit and well-tended, with spacious, high-ceilinged flats commanding six-figure sums. In some ways, they are a throwback to Old Edinburgh and the towering, teeming buildings of the seventeenth and eighteenth centuries, when the city tried copying some of the housing-stock of Paris. One theory has it that the Old Town was a democratic living-space, in that rich and poor lived in the same tall structures, with the poorest in the eaves and the wealthy nearer ground-level, and that this democracy crumbled with the move of the bourgeoisie to the New Town at the end of the eighteenth century. In his historical overview *Edinburgh*, author Charles McKean says that the New Town 'brought to the surface Edinburgh's latent class-conscious-ness' and he goes on to quote the views of an American journalist, who visited in 1834: 'A more striking contrast than exists between these two parts of the same city could hardly be imagined . . . Paris is not more unlike Constantinople than one side of Edinburgh is unlike the other. Nature has properly placed a great gulf between them.'

This 'great gulf' being the Nor Loch, which was eventually drained to create Princes Street Gardens.

This sense of Edinburgh's inequalities features in most of the litera-ture to emerge from the city, including, most famously, *The Prime of Miss Jean Brodie*. The scene in which Brodie takes her young elite for a walk through the Grassmarket, there to pass by the city's great unwashed, could still be repeated today – not in the touristified Grass-market itself, but on the adjoining Cowgate, between the site of the Edinburgh gallows and the present-day mortuary. This mortuary has given me my share of problems over the course of the series. To help with the writing of *Strip Jack*, I asked an Edinburgh pathologist if I could put some questions to him. He agreed, and some time after our first meeting gave me a tour of the mortuary. By this time, I was priding myself on the realism in my books, but I wasn't sure my readers would believe a mortuary where tomatoes were grown on window-sills and a mannequin in coat and hat sat at a desk. The mortuary of my books remains a less lively place (if you'll pardon the expression) than its real-life counterpart. And when the mortuary closed for a time to facilitate the introduction of a new ventilation system, my fictional equivalent did the same. Maybe only a few dozen people in the city would have noticed, but it was important to me that they did.

I've made other changes to the city, too. I'm not overly keen on writing about real-life housing estates, especially when I'm using them in my stories as a base for terrorists or drug dealers. Edinburgh is ringed with 'problem' estates which remain unvisited by most, and unseen by tourists. This is one reason they remain a problem: out of sight, out of mind. Progress, however, is ongoing, and instead of denigrating these real communities I would rather invent housing schemes of my own, such as the Garibaldi Estate (from *Mortal Causes*), Greenfield (*Dead Souls*), and Knoxland (*Fleshmarket Close*). Rebus himself is able eventually to acknowledge that Edinburgh's real-life estates are not all bad:

Danny Simpson lived at home with his mother in a terraced house in Wester Hailes.

This bleak housing-scheme, designed by sadists who'd never had to live anywhere near it, had a heart which had shrivelled but refused to stop pumping. Rebus had a lot of respect for the place. Tommy Smith had grown up here, practising with socks stuffed into his sax, so as not to disturb the neighbours through the thin walls of the high-rise. Tommy Smith was one of the best sax players Rebus had ever heard (*The Hanging Garden*).

In this case, I named the real housing-scheme because it was going to play no further role in the drama, and because I wasn't being nasty about it. The story about Tommy Smith is true, and everyone in Edin-

OPPOSITE: Inside the mortuary.

I often describe the Cowgate as a chasm. This photo, taken from the Cowgate, shows why.

burgh who knows his work also knows where he grew up – so why tinker with the facts?

Rebus's city, however, comes alive at night. This is when Jekyll most conspicuously becomes Hyde:

> He walked up the Bridges, stopped at some railings so he could look down on to the Cowgate. There were clubs still open down there, teenagers spilling on to the road. The police had names for the Cowgate when it got like this: Little Saigon; the blood bank; hell on earth. Even the patrol cars went in twos. Whoops and yells: a couple of girls in short dresses. One lad was down on his knees in the road, begging to be noticed.
> Pretty Things: 'Cries from the Midnight Circus' (*Dead Souls*).

And here is Robert Louis Stevenson over a hundred years before: 'To look over the South Bridge and see the Cowgate below full of crying hawkers, is to view one rank of society from another in the twinkling of an eye.' Same scene, and similar feelings, but with the peddlers replaced by drunks. The cultural commentator Stuart Cosgrove complained recently that too many of Scotland's creative artists concentrate on the downbeat and the negative in Scottish life, producing essentially glum, introspective and backward-looking works. He may be right. My own defence is that a detective would not deal on an everyday basis with happy shiny people. Crime fiction *can* be uplifting, but it deals in the main with human suffering – and suffering has always been of interest both to the artist and to his or her audience. I'm reminded of Virginia Woolf's comment on James Joyce's *Ulysses* that it was the work of 'a queasy undergraduate squeezing his pimples'. Many a pimple has been squeezed recently by Scottish writers, sometimes, I'd guess, in reaction to earlier novels such as *The Prime of Miss Jean Brodie* which seemed to deal with a class these new writers knew nothing of, or found redundant or exhausted.

Edinburgh, however, can contain multitudes. There is room both for the city of *Trainspotting*'s Begbie and the city of Alexander McCall Smith's *Sunday Philosophers Club*. There are also multiple crime writers at work today, their collective body-count outnumbering by far the body-count of the real city. Edinburgh doesn't seem to mind. In the early days, reviewers wrote of my work that it was unlikely to be recommended by the local tourist board. Yet there's now a successful walking-tour of Rebus's Edinburgh, mixing scenes from the books with snippets of local history and lore.

Sometimes I get things wrong, of course, and people are quick to correct me, such as when I misnamed the city's 'setts' as 'cobbles' or placed a foot-rail along the front of the bar in the Oxford Bar. Other times, I have to revise my estimation of an area. For example, Morningside is described in *Mortal Causes* as being 'that genteel backwater, where old ladies in white face-powder, like something out of a Restoration play, sat in tea shops'. Having moved to Morningside a couple of years back, I admit I've yet to see anything like this. There are cafés, but serving espresso to a mixed clientele, usually with trance music on the hi-fi and no sign of a doilie-draped cake-stand. I can always make the excuse that the error was Rebus's rather than mine, but on this occasion I'm willing to take the rap.

Edinburgh keeps evolving as a city, which means that some of the early novels already have a 'historical' feel to them. The near-uninhabitable tenements of Niddrie and Craigmillar, as described at the start of *Black and Blue*, have almost disappeared entirely to be replaced with hospitable housing. The waterfronts of Leith and Granton have been gentrified – or are at the planning stage. Infamous gap-sites such as the ones behind the Usher Hall and on the eastern side of Leith Street have been replaced with modern developments, and a stretch of Lothian Road has been transformed into the 'Financial District', complete with Sheraton Hotel and Spa (as mentioned in *Set In Darkness*). Joyce once said of *Ulysses* that if Dublin were blown to kingdom come, it could be rebuilt using his book as the blueprint. Yet after fifteen full-length novels, I'm not sure the same can be said for my version of Edinburgh. In some ways (and ironically, given their alleged mutual antipathy), we have Glasgow to thank for this. When the 'second city of the Empire' was elected European City of Culture and began its 'Glasgow's Miles' Better' campaign, it began a radical programme of regeneration. Edinburgh was slow to follow, but follow it did. How far a UNESCO World Heritage Site can move with the times is a moot point. I've no doubt

that Rebus would see modern architecture (and art . . . and music . . .) as a series of carbuncles, and he would be in good company.

In fact I've often hidden behind Rebus when offering criticism. For example, in *Strip Jack* Rebus investigates a case at the university, and sees some of the buildings around George Square through his creator's eyes:

Some Edinburgh setts, this time in Leith.

On one side of Buccleuch Place sat a row of neat tenements, owned by the university and used by various departments. The Professor called it Botany Bay. And across the road uglier shapes reared up, the modern stone mausoleums of the main university complex. If this side of the road was Botany Bay, Rebus was all for transportation.

It was actually an eccentric tutor of mine, Mac Emslie, who used the 'Botany Bay' phrase, meaning by it that those staff members consigned to Buccleuch Place were kept distant from the hub of their departments. My own main complaint against the ghastly 1960s buildings was that they seemed to produce a wind-tunnel effect whenever a strong breeze arose. You'd have to fight your way up steps or around corners, exhausted by the effort. A lecturer was once blown over by the wind, as was my Aunt Jenny on one of her pilgrimages to Jenners department store. There have probably been dissertations written on the extent to which climate influences communities. Robert Louis Stevenson, who was eventually to settle in Samoa, didn't think much of Edinburgh's climate:

Edinburgh pays cruelly for her high seat in one of the vilest climates under heaven . . . The weather is raw and boisterous in winter, shifty and ungenial in summer, and a downright meteorological purgatory in the spring.

Which translates in the Rebus series as:

Springtime in Edinburgh. A freezing wind, and near-horizontal rain. Ah, the Edinburgh wind, that joke of a wind, that black farce of a wind. Making everyone walk like mime artists, making eyes water and then drying the tears to a crust on red-nipped cheeks' (*Strip Jack*).

Crossing the Meadows in winter.

Some people said the weather made the Scots: long drear periods punctuated by short bursts of enlightenment and cheer. There was almost certainly something to the theory. It was hard to believe this winter would end, yet he knew that it would: knew, but almost didn't believe   (*Let It Bleed*).

Considering that I was living in south-west France when I wrote these passages, they show the effect Edinburgh's weather had on me, the memories fresh and painful. During all my time as a student, I never lived closer to the university than Marchmont, a fifteen-minute walk which, in winter's blasts, could feel like an eternity. I had two stints in the New Town, and would walk from there, too, a steep uphill climb and a half-hour tramp to lectures and tutorials. When I write about the Edinburgh weather, I write from experience. There is something in Rebus, however, that relishes these challenges, seeing them as another test sent from a cranky God:

The sun was out, bathing the tired buildings in dazzling light. Edinburgh's architecture was best suited to winter, to sharp, cold light. You got the feeling of being a long way north of anywhere, some place reserved for only the hardiest and most foolhardy   (*Let It Bleed*).

In another book, Siobhan comments that the weather on that one day has combined elements from four different seasons, to which Rebus responds that at least you get your money's worth in the Scottish climate. So have millennia of Caledonian weather made us what we are? It's true that the long winters can exacerbate feelings of depression. We stay indoors, drinking and watching TV. In ages past, it was said that one reason for the educatedness of the average Scot was down to long dark nights spent beside the fire with a good book. Not so true these days, and politicians agonise over our rates of literacy.

At the same time, men living in Glasgow will die on average a good ten years before their counterparts in south-west England. There appears to be a self-destruct gene in the Scottish lineage. We know how to change our diet, know that smoking, binge-drinking, and lack of exercise doom us to this early grave, yet we resist change. Maybe it's the influence of Calvinism again: aware of our mortality, we choose to enjoy life in our own way. We're addicted to that which destroys us. At one point in the series, Rebus sees alcohol, sugar and fat as the unholy trinity of the Scottish diet. Siobhan points up something similar:

> The Scots had an unenviable record for heart disease and tooth decay, both the result of the national diet: saturated fats, salt and sugar. She'd wondered what it was that made Scottish people reach for the comfort foods, the chocolate, chips and fizzy drinks: was it the climate? Or could the answer lie deeper, within the nation's character? (*The Falls*)

Will the projected smoking ban in bars and restaurants presage a slow but telling change in our attitudes? I hope so, though the fatalism inherent in many Scots will take generations to fade.

If the climate of Edinburgh has an effect on its denizens, what of the city's structural character? Can architecture also affect those who live with it? Charles McKean certainly thinks so:

> Embedded in its people's character are the contrasts of its very landscape: barely suppressed savagery beneath ordered respectability (*Edinburgh*).

It may be difficult to believe in 'suppressed savagery' among the takers of tea in Jenners' café, but Miss Jean Brodie showed just such emotions simmering always beneath the surface. Edwin Muir saw other emotions being repressed in the 1930s:

> This yearning again is drenched in unsatisfied sex. Nowhere that I have been is one so bathed and steeped and rolled about in floating sexual desire as in certain streets of Glasgow and Edinburgh (*Scottish Journey*).

Charles McKean, who says of post-Enlightenment Edinburgh that 'respectability had not obliterated bawdy . . . merely tidied it away', would almost certainly agree with Muir. Sexual dysfunction might well lead to the 'suppressed savagery' of Jean Brodie and her ilk, but class

and status have something to do with it, too. The building of the New Town's grid and circuses imposed upon Edinburgh a sense of decorum and order. It remains a city where one is supposed to know one's place. I was once invited to a meeting at the New Club, and was shown up to the meeting-room by one of the staff. A club member – the New Club, with its discreet entrance on Princes Street, is *the* meeting place for the Edinburgh establishment – stopped us on the stairs and commented on my lack of a necktie. At no time did he attempt eye-contact with me; his words were aimed at the staff member. When I started to explain that I'd brought a tie with me for just such an emergency, he ignored me completely and kept berating the poor lackey.

Such moments are telling.

On more than one occasion, a dentist's opening gambit, once I'm in the chair, has been to ask which school I went to. Edinburgh is a Scottish anomaly in the number of fee-paying schools it sustains (a quarter of all high school pupils is educated privately). My novel *A Question of Blood* was written in order to explore what this says about the city (even though I chose to place my school outside the city, so as not to invite comparisons with any real-life institution). The incidence of these schools, with their imputed elitism, strengthens the sense of Edinburgh as a divided city: haves and have-nots; the Protestant, Hearts-supporting west end, versus the Catholic, Hibernian-loving east end; New Town versus Old Town. For such a small place, Edinburgh can appear endlessly complex, which explains why I keep finding new things to say about it in my books. Here's museum curator Jean Burchill's take on the city:

Reticence was an Edinburgh tradition. You kept your feelings hidden and your business your own. Some people put it down to the influence of the Church and figures like John Knox – she'd heard the city called 'Fort Knox' by outsiders. But to Jean, it was more to do with Edinburgh's geography, its louring rock-faces and dark skies, the wind whipping in from the North Sea, hurtling through the canyon-like streets. At every turn you felt overwhelmed and pummelled by your surroundings. Just travelling into town from Portobello, she felt it: the bruising and bruised nature of the place   (*The Falls*).

LEFT: Jenners department store, Princes Street.

RIGHT: A world away from Princes Street.

One of the coffins from the Museum of Scotland, the inspiration behind *The Falls*.

Recently, the *Edinburgh Evening News* produced a facsimile of an edition from VE Day – Tuesday 8 May, 1945. A headline on page seven reads: EDINBURGH REJOICES, but is hastily followed by a sub-heading: 'Restrained Note In City's Response'. We're back to bridled Edinburgh, hidden Edinburgh, the aspects of the city I've tried to explore in my fiction. Luckily for me, Edinburgh has hidden structures and a secret history which can be used as metaphors for my journey. For example, when someone at the Museum of Scotland alerted me to a display of tiny coffins, I had the starting-point for *The Falls*.

The process of discovery is ongoing. It was reported in March 2005 that one of the historic closes on the Royal Mile was about to be reopened after years of neglect. Byers' Close sits opposite St Giles' Cathedral, in the most-visited part of the Old Town. I'd probably walked past it a few thousand times without being aware of it, hidden as it is behind a padlocked wooden door. It's extraordinary to think that something so public can also be so unknown, but that's Edinburgh for you, revealing itself only by the most reluctant of degrees.

But how then to explain the riotous assembly of the annual Festival and Fringe? Rebus, of course, hates those few weeks in August:

> The Edinburgh Festival was the bane of Rebus's life. He'd spent years confronting it, trying to avoid it, cursing it, being caught up in it. There were those who said that it was somehow atypical of Edinburgh, a city which for most of the year seemed sleepy, moderate, bridled. But that was nonsense; Edinburgh's history was full of licence and riotous behaviour . . . The High Street was packed with people, most of them just browsing. Young people bobbed up and down trying to instil enthusiasm for the Fringe productions they were supporting. Supporting them? They were probably the *leads* in them. They busily thrust flyers into hands already full of similar sheets . . . There were jugglers and people with painted faces, and a cacophony of musical disharmonies. Where else in the world would bagpipes, banjos and kazoos meet to join in a busking battle from hell?
> (*Mortal Causes*)

For years it was said that the denizens of Edinburgh actually packed

Edinburgh at Festival time.

OPPOSITE: Another kind of Tattoo.

up and left in August, renting their homes out to performers for astronomical sums. But with the advent of computerised booking for shows, it has now been proved that over half the tickets for the Festival as a whole go to local postcodes. Again, this is all too typical of Edinburgh: we don't want anyone to think we're enjoying ourselves or taking pleasure in our own city. When I was asked to write about the Festival for a book called *British Greats*, this was my conclusion:

> Edinburgh is a small city with large ambitions. For many years, it seemed insular and inward-looking, saddened by opportunities squandered and a parliament lost to London. In recent years, however, it has begun to feel a new confidence, a new and more vibrant sense of itself. At last, Edinburgh feels that it deserves the Festival. The word 'international' has seldom rung so sweetly in the city's ears.

A good deal of this new-found confidence, of course, is down to the parliament. Once amorphous, it now has its permanent HQ, nestling below Salisbury Crags, sandwiched between the Dumbiedykes housing-scheme and the Palace of Holyrood. That the character of Edinburgh is inherent in its landscape is validated by the lengthy arguments of a few years back concerning just where the parliament should be built. One potential site was dismissed by the ruling Labour party as 'a Nationalist shibboleth'. Another was not central enough. The bickering and point-scoring stopped when a brewery stepped in to offer a parcel of its land – the perfect solution.

My favourite story concerning town-planning happened, however, around the time of the construction of the New Town. A shopkeeper noted that the rubble from the building work might usefully be dumped in a mound which would link New Town to Old. This eventually happened, the resulting conduit named to this day The Mound. Unfortunately for the shopkeeper, however, the routing of The Mound entailed the demolition of his own premises . . .

In one book I call Edinburgh a 'conservation village' of half a million inhabitants. This sums up for me the difficulties faced by my home city in the twenty-first century. Edinburgh is thriving, and needs to thrive to survive. But if expansion means change, will the city's unique character be lost? It's a question I may yet tackle in the series, with Rebus once more my mouthpiece and explorer.

The Edinburgh Rebus patrols is mazey indeed, and treacherous with it. He sees the place as a series of connections: there are never many degrees of separation between the city of the dispossessed and that of the establishment. Beggars ply their trade outside the New Club, while city gents slip into the lap-dancing emporia of the 'pubic triangle' behind Lothian Road. Rebus, meantime, visits the dentist, and stares at an aerial photograph of the city on the ceiling above his head, mapping scenes from previous adventures:

> There's Calton Hill, where Davey Soutar ended up. There's St Leonard's . . . and Great London Road. Hyde's Club was just down there. Ooyah! There's Stenhouse, where Willie and Dixie lived. You could see Saughton Jail quite clearly. And Warrender School, where McAnally blew his head off. He had a sense of the way the streets interconnected, and with them the lives of the people who lived and died there. Willie and Dixie had known Kirstie Kennedy, whose Father was Lord Provost. McAnally had sought out a councillor as witness to his act of self-destruction. The city might cover a fair old area, its population might be half a million, but you couldn't deny how it all twisted together, all the criss-crossed lines which gave the structure its solidity . . . (*Let It Bleed*)

This then is Rebus's Edinburgh.

ABOVE: This weir at Dean Village
provided me with a book jacket.

RIGHT: HMP Edinburgh,
known to locals as Saughton Jail.

7

Outlands

WITH THE EXCEPTION OF *Tooth and Nail* (set almost entirely in London) the early Rebus novels did not stray far from Edinburgh. Even now, I'm conscious that most detectives do not travel hither and thither outside their normal territory. If a cop from Lothian and Borders Police has some questions that need asking in Wick, the usual procedure will involve a call to the nearest police station, where the 'locals' will be invited to take on the task. If a physical visit really is required, then preliminary negotiations will take place, the local squad being alerted to the forthcoming intrusion.

None of which has stopped me taking Rebus to Shetland, the Highlands, Aberdeen, Glasgow, the Borders, Fife, Dundee, Jura, rural Perthshire, Dundee, Clackmannan . . .

He can do this because he refuses to play by the rules. I started him off slowly, however, with that family visit to Fife at the beginning of *Knots and Crosses.* It would be novel number eight – *Black and Blue* – before he would really spread his wings. The thing was, I'd spent six books probing the machine that was Edinburgh. I was more confident as a result of this lengthy 'apprenticeship', and reckoned I could use my detective to explore Scotland a little more widely, especially as plenty of Scots would be only too happy to tell outsiders that Edinburgh isn't really representative of the whole country.

After Edinburgh itself, the place I write about most is Fife. Because I grew up there, Rebus's memories tend to be my own, whether he's recalling his mother scrubbing her doorstep with bleach (as in *Let It Bleed*) or thinking back to his childhood bedroom:

The bed feels like one he had as a kid, when a hot-water-bottle was all he had to keep the chill off, and mounds of gritty blankets, puffed-out quilts. Heavy and suffocating, tiring in themselves   (*Knots and Crosses*).

East Lothian.

The house Rebus grew up in was my own, and suffered the same problems. In winter, the condensation on the windows would freeze overnight. Lacking central heating, we relied on a paraffin-heater in the bathroom and a Calor heater in the living-room. There were mornings when I'd wake up with only my nose showing from beneath the bed-clothes:

Cardenden.

> When Rebus had been a kid, they'd eaten as a family in the kitchen, bringing out the fold-down table. But in later years, Rebus senior had hauled the table into the living room, so he could eat near the fire and the television. A two-bar electric heater warming his back. There was a Calor gas heater, too. It always steamed up the windows. And then, overnight in winter, the condensation would freeze, so you had to scrape it off in the morning, or mop it with the kitchen flannel once the heating got going (*Set In Darkness*).

My mother used a wringer and a double-sink to do the family's wash-load until around 1970. At around the same time, we got our first telephone. A few years later came a colour TV (this last rented from the Co-op). In one book, Rebus heads back to Cardenden and wonders if the memories will be sweet or sour. Passing a Chinese Carry-Out, he finds his answer: both, naturally.

> He passed Loch Leven (scene of many a family picnic when Rebus had been a kid), took a right at the next junction, and headed towards the tired mining villages of Fife. He knew this territory well. He'd been born and brought up here. He knew the grey housing schemes and the corner shops and the utilitarian pubs. The people cautious with strangers, and almost as cautious with friends and neighbours. Street-corner dialogues like bare-knuckle fights. His parents had taken his brother and him away from it at weekends, travelling to Kirkcaldy for shopping on the Saturday, and Loch Leven for those long Sunday picnics, sitting cramped in the back of the car with salmon-paste sandwiches and orange juice, flasks of tea smelling of hot plastic (*Strip Jack*).

St Andrews.

My parents took me to Loch Leven, too, though we owned no car and were dependent on Aunt Jenny to drive us there. Yes, we shopped in Kirkcaldy (and I would shoplift there, too, in time). But I don't just share my memories with Rebus. In *Knots and Crosses* the villain of the piece recalls his fear of crossing a pipe which spanned a river. I had that same fear of a pipe across the River Ore. Sometimes I had to sit down and slide my way over it on my backside. Other times, I would jog to the nearest bridge, catching my friends up eventually, feeling embarrassed by my failure. Likewise, the family history of Janice Mee (Rebus's old flame from schooldays) in *Dead Souls* mirrors my own family. Rebus himself remembers visiting relatives in Methil and Aberdeen (my own uncles and aunts), and recalls his father taking him to watch Cowdenbeath FC matches (as my father did – even when the home game featured the reserves rather than the first team).

In the summer, we would rent a caravan in St Andrews for a couple of weeks. A steep path led from the caravan site to the beach, and there was a deep drainage-hole there that terrified me as a five-year old. A few years ago, I returned to St Andrews to write about it for a newspaper, and was amazed to find the hole still there, if not exactly such a daunting prospect to walk past. In *Set In Darkness*, Rebus, too, revisits the same path:

'Christ, it's still here!' He stood looking down. The hole had been fenced off from the path; didn't seem half as deep. But this was definitely the same hole . . . 'This thing scared me half to death when I was a kid. Cliffs to one side and this on the other . . . I had nightmares about this hole!'

There's much to be said for writing as an act of therapy.

Apart from those holidays in St Andrews, my family barely traversed Scotland. There were very occasional trips to Edinburgh, and one driving holiday which took us as far as Aberdeen and Ullapool. My mother took me on a day-trip by train to one of the towns on the Clyde, but it left no discernible impression. As a sixteen-year old, I turned down the chance to go to concerts in Glasgow, which meant missing out on the likes of Frank Zappa. But Glasgow was too far; an alien land populated by people whose accent I would struggle to understand, and whose dialect would seem as alien as Vulcan.

OVERLEAF: Glasgow.

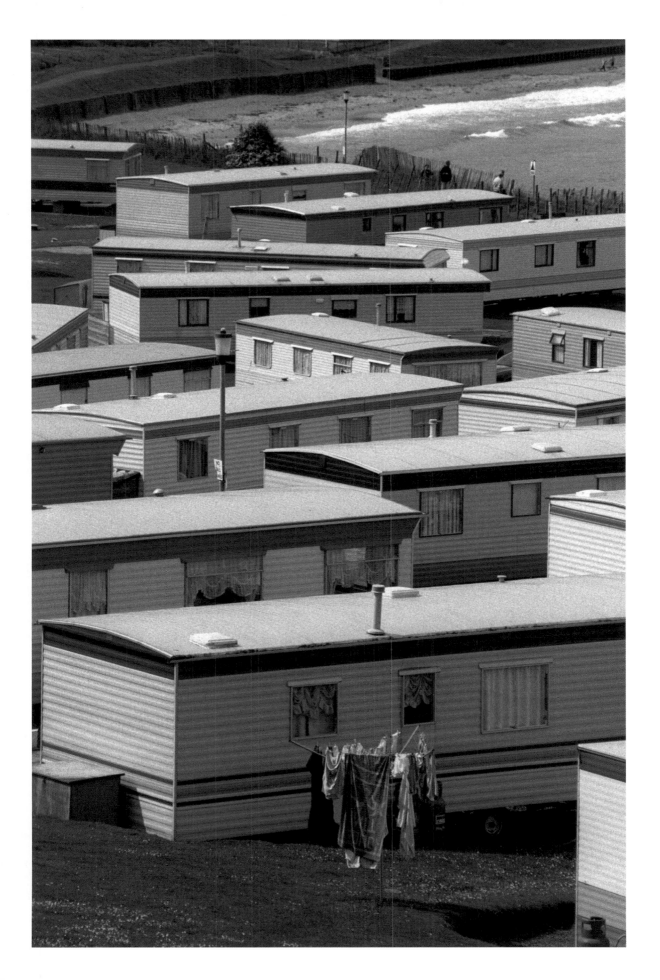

Readers have pointed out that Glasgow gets a raw deal in the Rebus novels. I explain to them that it's not my fault. Cops mistrust colleagues even within their own division, so the chances of Rebus having friendly relations with Strathclyde Police were always going to be remote. And the antipathy between the two cities stretches back through history. The antagonism noted by Edwin Muir in the 1930s – 'ridiculous in essence, jocular in expression and acrid in spirit' – survives to this day. Visitors who come to Scotland aware of this constant sparring between the country's two main cities are often perplexed by their geographical proximity to one another. It's not like London and Manchester or New York and Los Angeles – barely forty miles separates the two Scottish cities. A train takes less than an hour, a car journey much the same. Yet Edinburgh and Glasgow seem so different in so many ways:

> Scotland's two main cities, separated by a fifty-minute motorway trip, were wary neighbours, as though years back one had accused the other of something and the accusation, unfounded or not, still rankled   (*Black and Blue*).

> He began to walk, not very sure in which direction he was headed. The city centre was laid out American-style, a grid system of one-way streets. Edinburgh might have its monuments, but Glasgow was built to monumental scale, making the capital seem like Toytown (*Black and Blue*).

If Edinburgh is Toytown, then Glasgow in the books is 'Weegie Land' (weegie being a shortened form of Glaswegian) or 'Raintown' (a reference to the title of Deacon Blue's first album). Not that Rebus is always disparaging of the place. From the late-1970s on, Glasgow went to great lengths – and spent a lot of money – improving its reputation. For one year it became European City of Culture, while banners and advertisements advertised Glasgow as being 'Smiles Better' – by which, presumably, they meant better than dour old Edinburgh. Outward appearance has always been important to Glaswegians: the city sported facial tans, designer clothes and trendy haircuts long before Edinburgh. There's an outgoing confidence to many Glaswegians that is harder to find in the capital. Some say it's because Glasgow is Scotland's true capital – twice the size of its east-coast neighbour. In the nineteenth century, when Glasgow was 'the second city of the Empire', a great industrial and trading centre, the so-called Tobacco Lords travelled to Edinburgh in a display of moneyed swagger. Edinburgh had the trappings of government, but these made it a Washington DC or a Canberra. Glasgow was New York or Sydney – so much more vibrant and interesting.

Then there's the fact that Glasgow is a celtic city, settled by migrants from Ireland. They brought religious tensions with them, but also brought that sense of lively engagement with society – what the Irish still call the 'craic' or 'crack'. Rebus himself is not slow to see that Glasgow has its plus points:

> Glasgow was changing. Edinburgh had grown corpulent these past few years, during which time Glasgow had been busy getting fit. It had a toned, muscular look to it, a confident swagger rather than the drunken stagger which had been its public perception for so long.
>
> It wasn't all good news. Some of the city's character had seeped away. The shiny new shops and wine bars, the bright new office blocks, all had a homogenous quality to them . . . Not that Rebus was grieving; anything was better than the old swampland Glasgow had been in the 50s, 60s and early 70s. And the people were more or less the same: blunt, yet wonderfully dry in their humour (*Tooth and Nail*).

Again, my problem in taking Rebus out of Edinburgh is that he tends to make business trips only, and his business is human cruelty and suffering. So it's not always realistic for me to have him smell the flowers along the way, or notice how pretty a certain town or village is. His professional cynicism clouds his vision. Here he is on a rare visit to the Borders:

> Whenever John Rebus had cause or inclination to drive through any town in the Scottish Borders, one word came to his mind.
> Neat.
> The towns were simply laid out and almost pathologically tidy. The buildings were constructed from unadorned stone and had a square-built no-nonsense quality to them. The people walking briskly from

Winter in the Debatable Lands.

bank to grocer's shop to chemist's were rosy cheeked and bursting with health, as though they scrubbed their faces with pumice every morning before sitting down to farmhouse fare. The men's limbs moved with the grace of farm machinery. You could present any of the women to your own mother. She'd tell them you weren't good enough for them.

Truth be told, the Borderers scared Rebus. He couldn't understand them. He understood though, that placed many more miles from any large Scottish conurbation than from the English border, there was bound to be some schizophrenia to the towns and their inhabitants (*Mortal Causes*).

These are what's called 'the Debatable Lands', so-called because the border between England and Scotland was constantly shifting, prior to the Act of Union. The Borders gave Scotland many of its ballads, filled with heroes and their exploits, along with a blithe belief in the supernatural, notably the Devil. From this oral tradition sprung everything from Muriel Spark's early fiction to the stories my father told me when I was a child. My own early books deal with devilry, especially so in *Hide and Seek*. The occultist introduced in that book, Matthew Vanderhyde (note the final four letters of his surname), would reappear in future stories, most notably *The Black Book* and *Mortal Causes*. In similar vein, the mystery surrounding a cache of tiny coffins would, in *The Falls*, take Rebus from a witchcraft display at the Museum of Scotland to Rosslyn Chapel in Midlothian. I first went to the village of Roslin (why the two have different spellings I'm not sure) in the late-1980s, when I was resident at the writers' retreat based within Hawthornden Castle. The chapel fascinated me, with its various mysteries and Knights Templar associations. (The original cover of *Resurrection Men* shows a templar gravestone in the village of Temple in Midlothian.) Rebus first visited it in *Set In Darkness*:

Roslin was the home of the ancient and extraordinary Rosslyn Chapel, which in recent years had become the target of a range of millennialist nutters. They said the Ark of the Covenant was buried beneath its floor. Or it was an alien mothership.

The nutters are back again now, of course, seeking the truth of *The Da Vinci Code*. Sadly they won't even find the scrap of paper I placed at the Apprentice Pillar as a clue for Siobhan to find in *The Falls*. That clue, like *The Da Vinci Code*, remains a piece of fiction.

Sometimes I'll use a location because I know it from past visits (for example, the brief mentions of Dunfermline in *The Falls*, or Nairn – where my family holidayed one summer – in *Dead Souls*). Other times, the choice of location is necessary in terms of a book's wider theme. This is certainly true of *Black and Blue*. In discussing the effect (notional and real) of the oil industry on Scotland, I could not ignore Aberdeen and Shetland – the two places most affected by that industry. Rebus had been to Aberdeen before in the series. Like me, he had an aunt who lived in the shadow of Pittodrie, and he visits her in *The Black Book*. She is deceased by the time an oil-worker's gruesome death causes Rebus to revisit the 'Granite City' in *Black and Blue*.

Growing up in Fife, Aberdeen had an almost talismanic quality to it. The one-time fishing-port had come to resemble El Dorado in the minds of unemployed Fifers, men used to the hard work of the coal-mines and who reckoned they could endure the hardships of off-shore toil. The media played its part, stirring a brew of stories in which men made (and spent) fortunes, hookers prowled the packed hotels and casinos, and roughnecks brawled in the streets. I visited Aberdeen and its satellite towns several times for research purposes – and even tried writing a screenplay about the oil industry (casting my unemployed Fifers as latter-day 'Boys from the Blackstuff'). Eventually, my own thoughts and feelings would become Rebus's:

For all the associations with granite, Aberdeen had a feeling of impermanence. These days it owed almost everything it had to oil, and the oil wouldn't be there for ever. Growing up in Fife, Rebus had seen the same thing with coal: no one planned for the day it would run out . . .

Rebus recalled the early oil years, the sound of Lowlanders scurrying north looking for hard work at high wages . . . You sat in Saturday afternoon pubs in Edinburgh and Glasgow, the racing pages folded open, dream horses circled, and spoke of the great escape you could make. There were jobs going spare, a mini-Dallas was being constructed from the husk of a fishing-port. It was unbelievable, incredible. It was magic.

People watching JR scheme his way through another episode found it easy to fantasise that the same scenario was being played out on the north-east coast . . . For working-class males based south of Aberdeen, it seemed like the word made flesh, not just a man's world but a hardman's world, where respect was demanded and bought with money. It took only weeks for the switch: fit men came back shaking their heads, muttering about slavery, twelve-hour shifts, and the nightmare North Sea.

And somewhere in the middle, between Hell and El Dorado, sat something approximating the truth, nothing like as interesting as the myths   (*Black and Blue*).

The fish market, Aberdeen.

I've quoted this section at length to show that sometimes it's the mood or the mythology of a setting that's important to the book. Rebus cannot hope ever to understand Scotland by concentrating on geography, scenery and architecture alone. It is the interaction between these and the people he investigates that will begin to provide some answers. When he flies from Aberdeen to Shetland, he becomes immediately aware both that he's a long way from home and that the islands' inhospitable climate will have left its mark on its inhabitants: 'the Edinburgh wind was a pro; sometimes you walked out your front door and it was like being punched in the face. But the Shetland wind . . . it wanted to pick you up and shake you.'

I'm conscious that I wrote those words without having visited Shetland. I was living in France during the writing of *Black and Blue*, and had managed a few trips back to Scotland for research, but it wasn't until I was back in the Dordogne that I realised Rebus needed to visit the Sullom Voe oil terminal. So I found some books about Shetland instead, and used those as my guides. A few years afterwards, I visited the Shetland Literary Festival with my family, and took Rebus's drive from the airport to Sullom Voe. It seemed to me I hadn't done too bad a job (certainly, I'd received no complaints from Shetlanders in the intervening years). I did hear, however, that the boatman who takes visitors to the island where

the ancient fort called Mousa Broch is sited, had perused my book and was left wondering how I'd managed to visit the place without his help.

Praise indeed.

The Rebus novels have given me the chance to explore Scotland. Unfortunately, my destinations are more likely to be prisons and housing schemes rather than romantic lochs. By the time of *Set In Darkness*, I had been able to tour Barlinnie Prison on the outskirts of Glasgow. When I describe its interior in that book, I'm speaking from experience rather than imagination. It's only when I make mistakes that I fall back on the old excuse: 'it's a work of fiction, not a travel guide.' (I have a friend who was a great fan of Frederick Forsyth until he described a phone-box outside a Tesco store in Saffron Walden; she lived there and knew no such phone-box existed . . .) Having taken Rebus to a real-life police station – St Leonard's – in *The Black Book*, it took me until *The Hanging Garden* to get its interior details right (due to a visit there to make a TV documentary). Likewise, I'd never been inside Rebus's second-floor flat on Arden Street until the *South Bank Show* took me there.

A north-east trawler.

In *Resurrection Men*, Rebus spends a lot of the book at the Scottish Police College at Tulliallan, on the outskirts of Kincardine. He does so because the Chief Constable of Lothian and Borders Police, reviewing a previous book in a Sunday newspaper, said that the only thing he didn't find credible about Rebus was his diet. The Chief's argument was that if Rebus drank, smoked and ate the way he does, he would be unfit and would be sent back to Tulliallan for re-training. I got in touch with the Chief Constable and said I would gladly take Rebus back to college . . . so long as he could fix it for me to visit the place. This he did, and *Resurrection Men* was the eventual result. One bonus of having Rebus travel between Edinburgh and Kincardine was that I could describe the oil refinery at Grangemouth, which illumines the sky at night 'like some low-budget *Blade Runner* set'. One of my favourite bands, the Cocteau Twins, started life in Grangemouth – another reason to acknowledge the town.

Scotland, of course, has suffered more than its fair share of real-life criminal tragedies. There's a thesis to be written on why so many of Britain's most notorious serial killers have had a Scottish connection, while two towns' names continue to resonate around the world: Dunblane and Lockerbie. I know detectives and other professionals who worked one or the other of these cases, but I've never explicitly written about either – in a country the size of Scotland, some wounds take a long time to heal. On the other hand, novels can sometimes investigate questions and reveal human truths which any number of official enquiries and media articles would leave untouched. In *A Question of Blood* we learn that Rebus, like so many other cops from the Lothian and Borders force, was drafted to Lockerbie. We find this out during a drive south which Rebus is making with a colleague, Bobby Hogan. Hogan spends much of the journey railing against his homeland: the weather, the traffic, the inbred sense of failure. This causes Rebus to take up a position unusual to him: he starts to defend Scotland. In particular, he feels that in the aftermath of the Pan-Am 101 disaster, the 'quiet dignity of the towns-people' in Lockerbie says more about the country than any number of negatives, and when he does take a rare break from a case – as when he takes Jean Burchill for a weekend on the west coast – he allows himself glimpses of a lush and vibrant Scotland:

> The grass was damp with dew underfoot, and there were thick grey clouds overhead. Yesterday's distant views across the loch had disappeared into the mist. They walked anyway. Jean was good at recognising birdsong. She knew plant names, too. Rebus took deep lungfuls of the air, reminded of childhood walks in the countryside around his home village in Fife, coal-mines co-existing with farmland (*Resurrection Men*).

In likewise fashion, Edinburgh must co-exist with the green belt around it, and with the villages and towns which do not want their identities eroded by affiliation:

> East Lothian to him meant golf links and rocky beaches, flat farming land and commuter towns, fiercely protective of their own identities. The area had its share of secrets – caravan parks where Glasgow criminals came to hide – but it was essentially a calm place, a destination for day-trippers, or somewhere you might detour through on the route south to England. Towns such as Haddington, Gullane and

North Berwick always seemed to him reserved, prosperous enclaves, their small shops supported by local communities which looked askance at the retail-park culture of the nearby capital. Yet Edinburgh was exerting its influence: house prices in the city were forcing more people further out, while the green belt found itself eroded by housing and shopping developments. Rebus's own police station was on one of the main arteries into town from the south and east, and over the past ten years or so he'd noticed the increase of rush-hour traffic; the slow, pitiless convoy of commuters   (*The Falls*).

I said earlier in this book that I started writing about Edinburgh – and by extension Scotland – to make sense of my surroundings, but I also wanted to show tourists and outsiders that there was more to these places than shortbread and tartan, golf and whisky and castles. Scotland faces the same challenges as any other nation. We worry about crime, the environment, education and health, employment and migration (in some years, Scotland loses more residents than it gains). Lacking confidence and battered by industrial decline, we've come to underestimate ourselves. I'm struck, however, that whenever Rebus travels around the country, he's as apt to comment on the strength of community spirit as he is to critique our perceived failings. At the same time, however, his class defines him, and he can feel awkward (despite shows of bravado) when socially out of his depth – as in the shooting-party scene in *Let It Bleed*. Rebus has been invited to the Perthshire estate of a senior civil servant, where he is introduced to some of Scotland's premier movers and shakers. He has no idea what he's doing there:

Ears still ringing, Rebus joined the others at the Land Rover. There were flasks of Scotch broth, sandwiches in silver foil, hip-flasks of whisky and larger flasks of tea. Rebus's sandwich was brown bread and smoked salmon. The salmon was sliced thick, and had been sprinkled with lemon juice and pepper. He took a small nip of whisky when the hip-flash came round, then drank two mugs of strong tea. With all the games he felt were going on, he wanted to clear his head. He wasn't sure if he was a player, a counter, or the die . . .

Practically every man present had it within his power to push Rebus off the playing-board and off the force . . .

The visit ends up being salutary, however, in showing Rebus another side of Scotland which had previously been hidden to him:

Scotland was a machine, a big machine if you looked at it from the outside. But from the inside, it assumed a new form – small, intimate, not that many moving parts, and all of them interconnected quite intricately.

In other words, Scotland itself is an extension of the aerial map Rebus perused earlier in the book, everyone and everything connecting. *Let It Bleed* concerns corporate and political corruption, tied to Scotland's desperate economic need for new industries to replace the old. Maybe that's why I decided that the central figure in the book – even though we see him only fleetingly – should be a dry-stane dyker, that most traditional and rural of jobs, but one which stands or falls (quite literally) on an expertise in the field of connectedness:

The man saw him coming, but didn't stop working. He had three piles of stones close to him, varying in sizes and shapes. He would pick one up, feel it, study it, then either put it back in the pile or else add it to the wall. And with a fresh stone placed in the wall, a new challenge presented itself, and he had to study his mounds of stones all over again. Rebus stopped to catch his breath, and watched the man. It was the most painstaking work imaginable, and at the end of it the wall would be held together by nothing more than the artful arrangement of its constituent parts.

Just like a police inquiry, Rebus himself might add.
Or a novel, his creator would be forced to rejoin.

8

An Attitude of Mind

THE PHOTOS IN THIS BOOK were taken by Ross Gillespie and Tricia Malley. I first encountered their work when I was asked to submit a short story to *Edit*, the in-house magazine of Edinburgh University. The story I wrote was called 'The Acid Test', and though it was set in the present and featured Rebus, it concerned a murder which had happened in the nineteenth century, in a tunnel beneath the university's original campus (now known as Old College). A month or so after submitting the story, I was taking part in a BBC radio documentary about Burke and Hare, and part of the programme took place in a passageway beneath the administrative offices in Old College. Not only was my imagined tunnel real, but it was how bodies were brought into Old College for dissection by the medical faculty – Burke's own corpse being one such.

Just one more coincidence.

Leith Docks.

A further couple of months passed before the magazine arrived at my home. The photograph used to illustrate it excited me immediately. It showed a shadowy figure walking into the Old College quadrant, and had been taken by the university's own photographers, Ross and Trish. I liked it so much, I sent it to my publisher in London. We were already using moody black and white photos for my jackets, but these were sourced from a photo library. Ross and Trish gave permission for us to use their 'Acid Test' photo on the original paperback jacket of *Dead Souls*, and provided another of their Old College pictures to grace the hardcover of *Set In Darkness*. It was to prove the beginning of a fruitful relationship. For the paperback of *Set In Darkness* they shot Queensberry House itself (not only the scene of the crime in that novel, but also home to the nascent Scottish Parliament) – for the first time, story and jacket photo meshed. For *Resurrection Men* they went to the

village of Temple and found a Knights Templar gravestone. *The Falls* would feature a weir on the Water of Leith at Dean Village (close to the scene of that book's climactic chase scene). The hardcover of *A Question of Blood* was shot at Port Edgar marina in South Queensferry (where one of the main characters in the story keeps a boat), while the paperback originally showed a close-up of a padlock on a boat-shed. Eventually, they would take new photos for some of my earlier books, including *Hide and Seek* (a playground near the Meadows) and *A Good Hanging* (a car park in the Old Town).

All of which led to the idea of a photographic book charting Rebus's Scotland, with text supplied by me. This gave me the opportunity to re-read all the Rebus books: not something I'd attempted before. Authors seldom read their own work: by the time a book has been published, we're busy with our next project. When a story is done, it's done – reading it through would only make most authors want to tinker with it. Having said that, I enjoyed the majority of the Rebus novels. *Knots and Crosses* I thought wildly overwritten – definitely a young man's book. *Dead Souls* possesses too many characters and story-lines: at points it confused even its author! But several books which had seemed real chores to write surprised me with their deftness – *Set In Darkness* and *Let It Bleed* especially. (I think they'd probably seemed chores because of the amount of political detail they had to embrace – it's never easy to make politics seem exciting to the layman.)

During the process of re-reading, I was amazed to find how much of my own life infiltrates the lives of my characters. In *Resurrection Men*, Siobhan thinks about how she crashed her car once at Tollcross. It was actually *my* first crash. In the novel, the car in question is a recent gift from her parents – in real life, it was a Renault 5 borrowed from my Aunt Jenny, who didn't know I planned to use it for a liaison in St Andrews (yes, in a caravan). In another book, Rebus remembers his childhood pets, which were actually my childhood pets, right down to the absconding tortoise. Meantime, some of Brian Holmes' experiences of London and university life are taken wholesale from my own, and when Rebus, at his father's behest, touches his dead mother's forehead, he does so because my own father did the same thing with me, so that I would never feel the need to fear dying or the deceased.

The above being the case, it also follows that my characters' often contradictory views of Scotland past and present will mirror my own feelings. Rebus and Siobhan both feel like outsiders in their own culture, while I grew up feeling 'different' from my family and friends, and trying desperately to blend in. It wasn't really until I left Scotland in 1986 that I felt compelled to analyse my own mixed feelings for my homeland. As a result, my novels grew more complex, more politicised. I started to ask questions about the nature of Scottishness – a state of mind most Scots probably take for granted. I've found no easy answers in my books – few answers at all, really. But that doesn't mean the questions don't need to be addressed. The themes I use in most of my books place questions in the minds of their Scottish readers: who are we, where do we come from, how do we feel about racism, sectarianism, Anglophobia, identity, the political process, our place in the wider scheme of things? These debates are continuing, and some of their conclusions may lie within the remit of the new parliament. Devolution has been centuries in the making; here's hoping it provides leadership and a newfound self-confidence. The habits of several lifetimes will be changed only with unceasing effort, but that effort will surely be worthwhile.

And Rebus's Scotland will have ceased to exist.

As well as reading my own work in preparation for the current volume, I also consulted my extensive diaries. From my pre-teens until I reached thirty, I kept a page-a-day diary, so was able to flick back through years of uncertainty as a fledgling writer. My time as a student in Arden Street was especially trying – for my friends as much as me. As well as garnering a slew of rejection letters, I would treat visitors to lengthy recitals of my latest scribblings. I remember late one night ploughing through a futuristic tale called 'Prey', only marginally aware that my friends' eyes were glazing over. On a different occasion, I allowed another friend an exclusive preview of my latest typescript, a contemporary story called 'Colony' (named for the Joy Division song, I don't doubt). She handed it back eventually with the telling words: 'Ian, you've mastered the art of writing beautifully on subjects of no particular consequence.' I almost took it as a compliment . . .

Thank God John Rebus sauntered into my head that winter's day,

bringing with him plots and themes and a voice people wanted to hear. All my life until that point, I'd been a writer with a yearning to be both published *and* popular. Back in Cardenden, my favourite (and best) school subject had always been English. Each week we would be asked to write an essay – in essence, a short story. I penned one such called 'Paradox'. The teacher liked it, but asked what relevance the title had. Answer: none at all. I didn't even know what a paradox was; but it was the title of a Hawkwind song, and I loved the look of the letters as I wrote them at the top of the page.

At the end of each school day, I would retreat home and pick up the *Dundee Courier*, attempting the 'quick' crossword with the aid of a small dictionary. In the evening, there would be games of Scrabble with my parents (they never complained about Roxy Music or Yes playing in the background). Words were the most important things in the world to me. They defined the space I lived in. The weekly purchase of *Sounds* or *New Musical Express* saw me digesting the small ads as well as every article and review. I would cut out my favourite pieces of writing and pin them to my bedroom wall. To paraphrase Rebus, talking of rock music: I didn't have much, but I had words.

And through words, I could create a universe.

So far in the Rebus series, I have written over one million words – many of them about Scotland. Have I come any closer actually to knowing the place? Maybe just a little. In re-reading my novels, I'm conscious of a question readers may well want answering: can crime fiction ever give a true and all-embracing account of a nation? The answer should be a resounding 'Yes!', but only if we include works by the likes of Dickens and Dostoevsky under the umbrella term of 'crime'. Crime itself does not define a country, though we can deduce much about a culture by the types and frequency of criminal activity found there, and by the culture's attitude towards crime and criminals. (What messages, for instance, do the incidence of gun crime and the reality of the death penalty send to people outside the United States?) In most regions of Scotland, crime remains low-level and controlled, which comes as little comfort if you're living in a housing-scheme overrun by vandals or a leafy suburb which is being targeted by housebreakers ('burglary' as a term does not exist in Scots Law – something I was told

The closer you get to the Forth Rail Bridge, the more complex it becomes.

OVERLEAF:

Shopping in Marchmont.

thankfully early in my writing career). At the same time, turn on the news or pick up any local newspaper and you'll see that crime is both widespread and a worry. An edition of the weekly *Dumfries and Galloway Standard* from April 2005 records school bullying, stabbings, assaults (including one on a police officer), the discharging of an air-gun, theft, drug-dealing, fraud, sexual assault, and vandalism, with many of the newspaper's reports emanating from trials at the Sheriff Court in Dumfries. No doubt newspapers from any other region in Scotland would flag up the same issues, for crime is part and parcel of our society. What crime writers can do is explore why crimes occur, what effect they have, and what they tell us about the world we've chosen to create for ourselves. Being such a (relatively) small and (relatively) self-contained country, Scotland can work as a microcosm for the wider world. As I found when I toured with my novel *Fleshmarket Close*, racism and immigration (both legal and illegal) are contentious issues in most western democracies. They are also issues which can be used to chart the changes in a nation's understanding of itself. As Rebus himself puts it:

> 'We're a mongrel nation, always have been. Settled by the Irish, raped and pillaged by the Vikings. When I was a kid, all the chip shops seemed to be run by Italians. Classmates with Polish and Russian surnames . . .' He stared into his glass. 'I don't remember anyone getting stabbed because of it' (*Fleshmarket Close*).

This fictitious stabbing took place on a tough estate called Knoxland, the name purposely evocative of John Knox and his followers, so that the estate itself becomes a microcosm of Scotland past and present, its various tower-blocks named after famous writers such as Burns and Stevenson, harking back to greatness as a lazy substitute for contemporary progress.

Edinburgh, too, has been used throughout the Rebus series as a microcosm of Scotland as a whole. The tensions which exist in Scotland, especially between progress and heritage, are found most readily in Edinburgh, a city sustained by tourism but for too long trapped in the past as a result.

I myself was slow to come to an appreciation of Scotland's natural heritage, and I'm still learning. In the summer of 2004, I went with my family on a driving holiday, with only the vaguest itinerary in mind. This was probably my most extended period of travel around my native land since a similar holiday when I was ten or eleven. What thrilled us most during this latest adventure were the unexpected moments: a two-car ferry plying the Cromarty Firth between Cromarty and Balnapaling; the stretch of perfect beach at Dornoch; the magnificence of the coastal road between Dounreay and Ullapool, mountains to one side and sea to the other; seals basking on the shore of Hoy. We stumbled upon Pennan, famous as the setting for *Local Hero* (itself a subtle dissection of the tension between tradition and commerce), and finished the trip with a weekend in Glasgow, complete with open-top bus tour and a sighting of Billy Connolly's 'big banana boots' at the People's Palace. Hard to imagine Rebus playing the tourist in Glasgow . . . or anywhere else for that matter. But maybe he's mellowing as he nears retirement, and that retirement could send him on his own tour around Scotland. Freed from his day job, it might be possible for him to get excited about his homeland, and to see its vast potential.

Driving through Cardenden recently, I stopped my car kerbside at the entrance to Ian Rankin Court. Families had moved into the houses. Gardens were being planted, bringing individuality to each abode. It struck me that nothing man-made defines a country – neither its artefacts nor its monuments. Golf, tartan and whisky fail to tell our story. A nation is defined by the very people who live there, whether they're in mansions or high-rises. They animate their surroundings and lay down markers. They breathe life into the place. If Scotland and Scottishness exist, they do so in the mind:

> Scotland's a sense of change, an endless
> becoming for which there was never
> a kind of wholeness or ultimate category.
> Scotland's an attitude of mind.

> (Maurice Lindsay, 'Speaking of Scotland')

Dunsapie Loch, part of Holyrood Park.

Portobello, home of one of
Rebus's lovers, Jean Burchill.

OPPOSITE: The Rennie Mackintosh
exterior of Glasgow School of Art.

A tenement stairwell,
Royal Mile, Edinburgh.

COLORS OF AFRICA